Linda —

Working together on the
Krumm genealogy has been
a pleasure. Enjoy the book,
keeping in mind that the
Wiedow and Krumm families
went to church together in
Germany (Eldena) and in
Iowa (Garnavillo).

— Ellen

# Who Wrote Those Letters?

In Search of Jürnjakob Swehn

by

Eldon L. Knuth

authorHOUSE™

*1663 LIBERTY DRIVE, SUITE 200*
*BLOOMINGTON, INDIANA 47403*
*(800) 839-8640*
*WWW.AUTHORHOUSE.COM*

First published by AuthorHouse 04/25/05

ISBN: 1-4208-3478-9 (sc)

Library of Congress Control Number: 2005902012

Printed in the United States of America
Bloomington, Indiana

This book is printed on acid-free paper.

The German-language version of this book, namely "Auf den Spuren von Jürnjakob Swehn," is published by MV Taschenbuch Verlag, Rostock, Germany.  Orders can be placed online at "Bestellung@mv-taschenbuch. de".

# Contents

# PREFACE

The central character of this book is an emigrant from Mecklenburg who arrived in Iowa in 1868 – in the middle of the second of three major emigration waves from Germany. At the age of 20, he was motivated to emigrate by a combination of economic opportunity in America and a desire to avoid military service in Mecklenburg. He described his experiences in letters to his schoolteacher in Mecklenburg, which letters were published in 1917 in a book [1] authored by one of the schoolteacher's sons. The book was a "best seller," with over a million copies sold to date and still selling well. A recent translation into English [2] is also selling well. But the identity of the letter writer was hidden behind a pseudonym. The present book reveals who really wrote those letters, and tells of the serendipity which made the discovery possible. Results of extensive researches detail his family background in Mecklenburg, a background which drove his decision to emigrate, and document how he and his family fared in this "land of unlimited opportunity."

This book is an historical document inasmuch as all names, places, dates and events are factual; no facts have been altered and no fictional material has been added. I am confident that the story which I tell here can be simultaneously factual and interesting.

Those parts of the book which describe the search for the identity of the letter writer are presented in chronological order; the book begins with my wife and I seated at a breakfast table in Germany in 1976, debating the wisdom of an impromptu visit to East Germany, and ends with my wife and I seated with German friends at a Cafe in the Schwerin Castle in 2002, reminiscing over the (sometimes unexpected) happenings of the prior 26 years.

Although a familiarity with the 1917 book of letters would add to your enjoyment of the present book, sufficient background is provided here so that you can enjoy this account of the search for the identity of the letter writer without going back to the original letters. This book would be especially appealing to you if you are one of the about 58 million U.S. residents who, according to the 1990 U.S. Census, can trace at least a part of their ancestry back to Germany.

These residents of German descent form the largest ethnic group in the USA. Most of them are descendants of the more than 5 million Germans who immigrated to America between 1683 and World War II. A large fraction of these came from northern Germany; after 1830, they emigrated mostly through Bremen, at the mouth of the Weser River, and Hamburg, at the mouth of the Elbe River. The emigrants left Germany in waves, with the crests corresponding to social and political crises in Germany. Major waves occurred in 1845-1858 (1.36 million emigrants), 1864-1873 (1.04 million emigrants) and 1880-1893 (1.78 million emigrants), where the counts are for emigrations to all parts of the world. What motivated so many people to turn their backs on their homeland and start new lives in strange and distant lands? And what were their experiences along the way?

German emigrations from 1683 until about 1820 were motivated by a combination of religious persecutions and economic hardships which followed the Thirty Years' War (1618-1648). After about 1820, the dominant reason for emigrating was a desire to improve one's standard of living – a want to escape from a society which offered no hope for a better life – a chance to start over in a "land of unlimited opportunity." An additional motivation for some males of military age was a means to avoid military service. The hopelessness which most of the peasants in Germany faced had its origin in the feudal system. Under this system the serfs were essentially slaves of the landowners. In 1820, Mecklenburg was the last of the Grand Duchies to free the serfs. But this did not help the workers. Although they were then free to go, the landowners were also free to let them go. Many of the former serfs had no work, and little opportunity to learn a new trade. It was nearly impossible for them to obtain their own cottages. Without housing, permission to marry usually was not granted by the landowners. The unemployed were a burden on the state and were sometimes encouraged by the state to emigrate. In 1846, crops failed in both Germany and Holland. Two years later, an attempted civil uprising in Germany failed. The plight of the workers motivated Fritz Reuter to publish his socially critical work, "Kein Hüsung" (No Housing), in 1857. These several factors combined to drive the 1845-1858 emigration wave. The following lull, from 1858 to 1864, was due in part to the 1857 Depression in the United States and the American Civil War (1861-1865).

The ensuing 1864-1873 emigration wave embraced three German wars, the Austro-Prusso-Danish War of 1864, the Prusso-Austrian War of 1866 and the Franco-German War of 1870-1871. The lull from 1873 to 1880 coincided with another depression in the United States, from 1873 to 1879. The 1880-1893 wave, which included also Poles and Jews, was driven largely by a combination of economic hardships, political problems and more affordable transportation. The decline in emigration after about 1893 was due largely to the industrialization of Germany. Since Mecklenburg was the last Grand Duchy to free the serfs, it is perhaps not surprising that emigration impacted Mecklenburg more than any of the other Duchies in Germany. After 1850, the fraction of the population leaving Mecklenburg was third only to that from Ireland and Galicia (what is now Poland and the Ukraine). One out of every three Mecklenburg residents left; 88 % of those leaving were from the rural areas.

Consider now the emigrations themselves – the routes which were taken, the ships which were used, and the experiences of the emigrants. The earliest emigration from Germany to America appears to have been in 1683; at the invitation of William Penn, 13 Mennonite families left from Bremen and settled in Germantown, PA. For the next century, the emigration rate increased relatively slowly; most departures were from Le Havre, Antwerp, Amsterdam and Rotterdam. A notable exception was the departure of 12,000 mercenary Hessian soldiers from Bremen in 1776; they fought on the side of the British in the American war for independence. After the end of the war, many of these soldiers (according to some estimates, about one-third) opted to stay in America rather than return to Germany.

After about 1830 the preferred point of departure shifted from Le Havre, Antwerp, Amsterdam and Rotterdam to Bremen. Dominant factors in this shift were the completion of the new harbor, including associated transportation links, at Bremerhaven in 1930 and the decree protecting passengers passed by Bremen in 1832. This 1832 decree required that the vessels be certified to be seaworthy, that passenger lists be submitted and that the ships carry provisions sufficient for 90 days when departing. In 1850 an Emigrants' House, which could provide lodgings and food for up to 3,500 people, was opened in Bremerhaven. From 1849 to 1893, 40 to 50% of all emigrants from Germany left through Bremen. It is estimated that, including all nationalities, about 7 million emigrants passed through Bremen headed for the New World.

In order to become competitive with Bremen, Hamburg enacted in 1837 a decree similar to the Bremen decree and founded in 1850 the Association for the Protection of Emigrants. In 1891 the emigrant flow through Hamburg surpassed that for Bremen. Emigration halls which could house 5000 emigrants waiting to board ship were built in 1901 and used until 1934. From 1850 to 1934, nearly 5 million, 37% of them German, passed through Hamburg; 82% of them went to the United States. From 1850 to 1940, 25 to 30% of the emigrants to America went through Hamburg. Although I have read that most emigrants from Mecklenburg left from Hamburg and that most emigrants from Pommern left from Bremen,

I find that most of the Pomeranians who settled in the county where I grew up left from Hamburg.

Most emigrants sailed directly to America; others sailed from Hamburg to Hull (on the east coast of England), then went by train to Liverpool where they boarded a ship for New York. Until the early 1890's, about 1/3 of the emigrants used the indirect (less expensive but more time-consuming) route.

Although the first ship to cross the Atlantic powered mainly by steam did so in 1833, steamships did not play a significant role in passenger traffic until the 1850's. For arrivals in New York: in 1856, less than 4% of the passengers were carried on steamships; in 1865, the number carried on steamships exceeded the number carried on sailing ships for the first time; and in 1873, less than 4% were carried on sailing ships. The last sailing ship carrying emigrants left Hamburg in 1879.

Sailing ships took an average of about 43 days for the trip from Hamburg to America. The steamships used in the late 1800's took 12 to 14 days. The ocean liners introduced in 1900 required only 7 to 10 days.

The time spent in either Bremen or Hamburg waiting to board a ship (frequently of the order of a week, sometimes more) was usually not pleasant. Local people frequently took advantage of the relatively unsophisticated emigrants. But the time aboard ship was the worst portion of the trip. Particularly early in the 19th century, overcrowding and sickness were commonplace. Typhus (ship fever), cholera and smallpox were common. In one voyage, more than 700 of 1267 passengers perished – most of "ship fever." In response to these conditions, the United States passed, at various times starting in 1819, legislation seeking to regulate the transport of passengers. For example, in 1848 Congress enacted a law which required ventilation of steerage quarters for ships carrying more than 100 passengers, a cooking range for every vessel carrying more than 50 passengers, a toilet for every 100 passengers and at least 14 square feet of floor space (2 feet by 7 feet?) for each passenger. Although these laws helped, overcrowding and sickness were nevertheless still commonplace. We have to admire our ancestors, including the central character of this book, who made the trip under these difficult conditions.

# Chapter 1

# LET'S SEE WHAT HAPPENS!

It was Saturday the 12th of June 1976. My wife, Margaret, and I were sitting across from each other at the breakfast table – in the very German apartment which had been our home for the past 9 months. We were both quite aware that this was our last weekend in Göttingen. My sabbatical leave, spent at a Max Planck Institute in Göttingen, had been good. I had found a research project which was of interest both to my host and to me, a project which was challenging but doable, and had a manuscript based on this work almost ready to send to my secretary at UCLA. I had presented a paper at a Symposium held at the Bodensee (Lake Constance) and we had attended a meeting of the von Humboldt Society (sponsor of my stay in Germany) in the Black Forest. On weekends, we had travelled to all corners of West Germany – including to the Oktoberfest in Munich and to Berlin. During the Christmas holidays, we had escaped the gray weather which is typical of Göttingen in the fall and spent a week in the Canary Islands. The Easter holidays we had spent in Venice. But it looked like politics and bureaucracy were going to rob us of a weekend which we had anticipated for months. We wanted to visit East Germany. For me, it was to be a pilgrimage to the land where most of my grandparents were born. For Margaret, it was to be an adventure suited to the "gypsy blood" in her veins. We had applied to an office located at the Alexanderplatz in East Berlin for a visa and accommodations in Schwerin – and had been told to apply in Hamburg. Applying to the office in Hamburg and receiving no response, I had called on the preceding Thursday to inquire about the status of our application. After a long delay during which I got the impression that the party at the other end of the line was looking for our application, I was told that no room was available in the Hotel Stadt Schwerin, the only hotel in Schwerin where foreigners were allowed to stay. We were very disappointed. For all I knew, this might be my last trip to Germany – my last chance to visit the land where Opa and Oma (Grandpa and Grandma) grew up. And if we don't go to East Germany, how do we spend our last weekend in Germany? In desperation I suggested that we simply drive to the border and "let's see what happens."

1

We hastily finished breakfast, put together enough luggage for two nights, checked our wallets, collected our maps for northern Germany, pocketed our passports and drove north out of Göttingen in the direction of the Horst border crossing near Lauenburg. Our minds were filled with uncertainty. Would we be allowed to cross into East Germany? And if we were, what would it be like? For lunch we decided to stop at a Gaststätte (restaurant) on the West German side – better to eat where we felt comfortable. We entered into a conversation with the owner – told him about our plans and anxieties. We mentioned that no-one knew about our plans; if we had difficulties returning, how would anyone in the west find out about it? The owner assured us that we would have no problem.

Our anxieties peaked at the border crossing. Since we had neither a visa nor hotel reservations, we were asked to pull out of line and park near a small office. However, what we were doing did not appear to upset them; as long as we had a passport and money (money for the visa, the hotel room and the mandatory conversion of foreign currency into East German currency), we appeared to be welcome. The process required that we temporarily surrender our passports, which raised our anxiety levels again. Making reservations for a room at the Hotel Stadt Schwerin was no problem. All was accomplished in about 20 minutes – we were sent on our way with visas, hotel reservations, East German currency <u>and</u> passports in hand – and with wishes for a good stay in East Germany! Why had it been so difficult to make the arrangements while in the West?

Now a strange new feeling arose. We had agreed to check in at the Hotel Stadt Schwerin, but no limitations had been placed on our travel route. No-one was following us. We appeared to be free to choose our route. But were they nevertheless checking on us? We must have been terribly obvious – driving a large 10-year-old Mercedes with Göttingen license plates on highways used otherwise sparingly by the diminutive and utilitarian East-German Trabants and Wartburgs!

We were reminded of an experience which we had on our return trip from Berlin. It was late in the night, it was dark, and it slowly dawned on us that we were essentially alone on the highway – that we were on an unfamiliar road. Much to our relief, we spied a lonely car parked at a Restplatz (resting place) on the side of the road. In response to my questions, the driver informed me that we were headed for the Polish border, that we needed to turn around, but that the next place where we could turn around was far away. The fuel needle pointed to 1/4 tank, indicating that we had a problem. Since the opposing lanes of traffic were separated only by a level grassy strip and no cars were in sight, I solved the problem by using this grassy strip to make a U-turn. A short time later I noticed in my rear-view mirror a blue flashing light. I ignored it. A short time after that – a siren. I stopped and offered my passport and driver's license to the officer. I hoped inwardly that the combination of an American passport, my German family name and my imperfect German would be in my favor. When asked why I hadn't stopped for the flashing light, I explained that I didn't realize that it was for me. When asked from where we had come, I replied "Berlin." He differed, saying that we were coming from Frankfurt (meaning the Frankfurt on the Polish border). I insisted that we were coming from Berlin. Then he informed me that I had made a U-turn. I very humbly agreed. He scolded, "Das ist streng verboten!" (That is strictly forbidden!) I explained that I had gotten lost and that I was low on fuel. He asked where I wanted to go, gave me directions and sent us on our way. I headed for the West German border, wondering to what extent the police had been checking on us prior to the officer stopping us.

Checking in at the hotel required that we once again temporarily surrender our passports. And when we got to our room, which we came to understand was on a floor set aside for foreign guests, we wondered how much of what we said was being monitored. Were we being paranoid – or were we being realistic?

From our room we had a view of the parking lot. Our car was obvious by its size in comparison with that of the Trabants and Wartburgs. (Fig 1.1). Several people were inspecting it – they appeared to be fascinated. I wondered if the distinctive Mercedes hood ornament would survive the trip. (It did.) We decided to take a ride and get acquainted with Schwerin. A short while into the ride, Margaret discovered that she was thirsty – so we stopped at a Gaststätte for a beer. We were the only customers; no chance for contact with local people. Since the weather was nice, we sat outside – in a garden-like setting. After finishing our beer, we strolled back to the car. Two people were inspecting it – a grandmother (Frau Ode) and her grandson (Andreas). More precisely, Andreas was inspecting it and telling Oma all about it. After a brief conversation, Frau Ode mentioned that her husband was nearby working in their Schreber-garten (a small garden, usually at the edge of a city, where city dwellers can grow their own fruits, vegetables and flowers). Would we like to meet him and see their garden? We jumped at the chance for more contact. It was only a five-minute walk. Their plot was one of many – all efficiently planted, healthy and productive. Herr Ode was tall, strong-boned and friendly – his handshake was that of a man who was used to working with his hands. The focal point of their garden was a one-room garden house, tiny but gemütlich (comfortable). It was complete with electricity, plumbing and room enough to sleep two. A small black-and-white TV set allowed them

3

to receive channels from the west. Herr Ode confided that plumbing was not really allowed, but that their son had arranged it for them. Here they could relax, away from the watchful eyes and ears of the city. He added, I thought a bit proudly, that he didn't worry much about what he said – he was retired now and the state couldn't do much to him.

Our conversations were open and candid. At one point in our conversations, I described my origins; although I lived now in California, I grew up in Iowa – in a neighborhood where most of the farmers had Mecklenburg origins. I mentioned that the farmers had maintained their buildings – they almost always looked freshly painted – and expressed my surprise that most of the buildings I had seen in East Germany appeared to be poorly maintained – they needed paint. What had happened? Herr Ode replied that the paint was now of such poor quality that painting was not worthwhile; good-quality supplies went to the Soviet Union. When I pointed out that their garden house looked freshly painted, he explained that their son had brought that paint back with him when he returned from a trip to Hamburg. He followed this explanation with two sobering conclusions which I will always remember: "We have lost our culture!" and "We are poor now!"

That evening, although we could have eaten at the hotel, we chose to eat dinner at a nearby restaurant. We wanted to experience the local atmosphere. We found the restaurant to be rather somber – everyone was minding his own business – there was no exchange of pleasantries between tables. After dinner we strolled through the neighborhood, taking in both the natural beauties (e.g., the Pfaffenteich, a picturesque small lake) and the shortcomings of the political regime (e.g., the lack of upkeep of the buildings). Then, rather than retiring to our austere room, we relaxed in the hotel lounge. In spite of my general feeling that contacts with East German citizens were frowned upon, I struck up a somewhat furtive conversation with a friendly local citizen. (I learned later that he was an off-duty dining-room waiter.) He introduced himself as Johannes and asked about my interest in Schwerin; I explained that I was born and raised in a part of Iowa which was populated largely by German immigrants from Mecklenburg and their descendants, and that indeed some of my ancestors stemmed from villages south of Schwerin. He asked if I had read the book "Jürnjakob Swehn" and, when I indicated that I had never even heard of the book, he brought a friend of his out from the kitchen. His friend explained enthusiastically that the book consisted of letters written to the schoolteacher (Gottlieb Gillhoff) in Glaisin, a village located south of Schwerin, by a former student (Jürnjakob Swehn) who had emigrated to Iowa. Upon asking where I could get a copy of the book, I was told that the book had not been available in East Germany since the coming of the DDR (German Democratic Republic) days. The book which the cook had read had been passed down in the family since pre-DDR days. Perhaps the East German government did not want the minds of their subjects swayed by stories of what is possible in a land which they were not allowed to visit! Since then I have heard also that in Nazi Germany certain chapters of the book, e.g., "On the Deathbed of my Mother" and "Jürnjakob, that is Homesickness," were favored above other chapters. To my surprise, Johannes indicated that a small party was planned for a little later at a nearby apartment, and asked if we would like to join them. In spite of our ongoing concern that such contacts were frowned upon, we accepted quickly – seeing the invitation as another golden opportunity to become acquainted with the East-German man-on-the-street. After a few more employees had completed their workday, we headed for the party – a couple of blocks from the hotel and up several flights of stairs. The party fare consisted of bread, cheese and wine; I wondered to myself how much of it was from the hotel. The guests included an individual from the entertainment field. I was surprised at how open this guest and Johannes were about their disenchantment with the DDR regime. During the evening, Johannes gave me his business card, on which he added his home address. We parted with the hope that we would meet again someday.

On Monday, before leaving Schwerin, we said Goodbye to the Ode grandparents. They apparently had taken a liking to us and presented us with a carved wall placque depicting the Schwerin Castle and with a bouquet of flowers cut from their Schreber-garten. As we left, Frau Ode pleaded with obvious emotions, "Please don't forget us!" I took her plea to include all of East Germany. On our way out of Schwerin, we stopped at a post office to mail postcards; I stayed in the car while Margaret mailed the cards. Moved to make a permanent record of the flowers while they were still fresh, I laid them on the dashboard and photographed them. Immediately a man approached the car and asked why I had photographed the nearby factory. I explained that the object of my photograph was the flowers on the dashboard. He differed, saying that I had indeed photographed the factory, ordered me to take no more photos and to leave the area. It was only then that I noticed that the factory was an agricultural plant for the production of fertilizer. My wife returned from the post office and we continued on our way back to the West German border.

## The Book

After returning to West Germany, I looked for the Jürnjakob Swehn book and was disappointed to learn that it was out of print. But I persisted and bought a copy when the first of numerous paperback editions appeared two years later [1]. When I showed the book to our very good friends, the Bossels, Liz challenged me with the comment that she would be proud of me if I finished reading it. I rose to the challenge and in the following months read the book as fast as my busy schedule and the writing style would allow. A charming part of the book is that Swehn lapses occasionally into Low German. Although we spoke Mecklenburg Low German at home when I was a child, my Low German is now rusty. I was pleasantly surprised, however, to find that my subconscious mind had retained much of the relevant vocabulary.

The book was published in 1917 and was an instant success. It appeared first in installments in the Tägliche Rundschau, a daily newspaper, in Berlin. By 1919, in spite of World War I (or were the sales enhanced by the war?), more than 100,000 copies had been sold. It was published in installments in German-language newspapers in the USA. According to the 1982 edition, 545,000 hard-cover copies and 29,000 soft-cover copies had been printed up to that time. It has been translated into Norwegian, Danish, Dutch and (relatively recently) English. In 1987, I had the privilege of speaking at a regional Iowa Genealogical Society Seminar in Elkader, Clayton County, Iowa and spoke on "Beyond the East German Wall!" I recounted, with the aid of slides, our visits to East Germany, focusing on our relatively extensive visit to the Mecklenburg and Vorpommern areas in 1986. In closing my talk, I asked how many had heard of the book. Although nearly 200 people were present, and most had lived all their lives in Northeast Iowa and had a keen interest in genealogy, no-one had heard of the book. This lack of familiarity with the book has been corrected now by the publication of the English translation [2] in the year 2000.

The father, Gottlieb Gillhoff, of the book author was born in 1832 in Glaisin and died in 1915 in Bremen [3]. He served as a teacher in the village school in Glaisin from 1854 until 1908. The son and author of the book, Johannes Gillhoff, was born in Glaisin in 1861 and died in 1930 in Parchim [4]. The father's tenure at the school spanned the era of the great emigration from Mecklenburg to America. Hartmut Brun [5] writes that, during the father's tenure, more than 350 persons emigrated from Glaisin and that the father exchanged letters with 250 of them. Although more than 80 years have passed since the first edition of "Jürnjakob Swehn, der Amerikafahrer" appeared in print, interest in the life and times of Jürnjakob

Swehn continues unabated. Indeed, during the last 10 years, interest has multiplied. The pocketbook version of the book, which appeared first in 1978, has gone through at least 16 editions. A symposium titled "Jürnjakob Swehn: Wahrheit und Legende (Truth and Legend)" was held in Spring 1993 at the European Academy on Lake Müritz in Mecklenburg-Vorpommern [6]. And Swehn was the central figure in the Internationale Fachtagung zur Migrationsgeschichte (International Symposium on Migration History) which was sponsored by the Johannes Gillhoff Society in June 1998 at Glaisin in Mecklenburg-Vorpommern. In a recent visit to the home page of the newspaper Schweriner Volkszeitung (http://www. svz.de), a computerized search for "Swehn" in the SVZ archives yielded 8 articles dealing with Swehn published over a four-year period. These articles summarize recent activities and publications motivated by the book.

## Swehn's Background

The motivations for Jürnjakob Swehn emigrating to America were typical of the thousands who emigrated at that time. His father was a day laborer; he could count on steady work only during the harvest season. Jürnjakob also was a day laborer and he expected that, if he stayed in Mecklenburg and regardless of how hard he or his children might work, he and his children would be day laborers all their lives; he would have little chance of ever owning his own home. He writes that he worked three years as a day laborer for a Hannjürn Timmermann in order to earn enough for his passage to America. While earning the money for his passage (29 Thaler), Jürnjakob dreamed of some day being economically free, of standing on his own land, and of owning his own home.

In one of the published letters, Jürnjakob wrote also that, in Germany, his family lived in a thatched cottage on the edge of the horseshoe-shaped village of Glaisin. (Figs. 1.2 and 1.3) It consisted of two rooms – a living room and a bedroom. The roof was so low that a tall person had to stoop under the rafters – unless he stood in one of the low places in the floor. The floor consisted of clay from the local hills; it looked nice on Sundays, when his mother scattered white sand on it. The potatoes were stored under a bed in the living room; there they would not freeze in the winter. Under the bed was also "room for a small pet pig." The walls were made of sticks interwoven with straw and covered on both sides with clay which had been mixed with chopped straw. The wind came through the walls, and in the winter they leaned straw bundles against the side of the cottage in order to help keep the snow out and the heat in. The cottage had only four windows;

one of them had been cracked as long as Jürnjakob could remember. The stove was made of firebrick covered with clay. Wood for the stove came from the nearby forest. The furniture was made by his father. On the walls were a mirror (with some of the silvered backing missing) and drawings of Christ on the cross and the Holy Genevieve.

## The Trip

The trip from Glaisin to New York is described in "The Crossing." He went by foot to Hamburg and by freight steamer to Grimsby, England. According to Jürnjakob, he left Hamburg on July 20, 1868. During the afternoon of the first day, the seas were so rough that all passengers were ordered below decks and the hatches were closed; all became seasick. That night, the seas calmed but the 85 oxen in the hold made such a stench that Jürnjakob spent the night up on the deck. From Grimsby, he went by train to Liverpool, where he had to wait for a sailship. He could not afford the luxury of a steamer; a sailship left Liverpool only every two weeks. He describes in detail the discomforts of the trip from Liverpool to New York, including the limited water supply, poor food (including worms in the meat), scabies, bed bugs and lice. However, on the 18th day out, Jürnjakob's meals improved greatly when he volunteered to replace the cook's helper, who had become quite ill. The crossing from Liverpool to New York took 7 weeks and 2 days, so that it seems likely that they arrived in New York about mid-September.*

Jürnjakob spent about a month outside New York City attempting to earn money toward his trip to Iowa. Since he was naive and not familiar with the farm tools and practices, it was a long month. People lied to him at least twice and stole from him at least three times. On the way back to New York City, he resolved that he would never allow people to take advantage of him again. He arrived back at the port with only one dollar in his pocket. Whether it was by accident or by plan, others from Glaisin, namely Schröder, Schuldt, Timmermann, Düde, Saß, Wiedow, Völss and Brüning, had arrived and congregated. They headed for Iowa, with Schröder loaning Jürnjakob the money for the trip.

*He arrived in New York aboard the Ceres on 14 Sept. 1868.
ELK

Fig. 1.1 Parking lot of the Hotel Stadt Schwerin viewed from our hotel room. As a result of the difference in size and design, our 1966 Mercedes was conspicuous during our entire stay in East Germany. The "creative parking" seen on the right-hand side of the lot is one driver's solution to the extreme scarcity of parking in Schwerin. (Photo by E.L. Knuth, 1976)

Fig. 1.2 Evangelical Lutheran Church, Eldena, Mecklenburg. Since Jürnjakob Swehn was from Glaisin, his family went to church here. (Photo by E.L. Knuth, 1986)

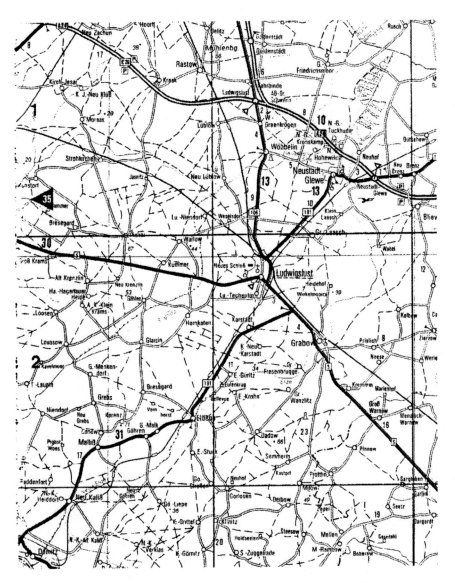

Fig. 1.3 Map of area in Germany where Jürnjakob Swehn lived prior to his emigration to America. He was born in Bellevue, went to church in Eldena, emigrated from Glaisin. Scale is about 4 miles per inch. (From Auto-Atlas Deutschland/Europa. Neuilly, France: Novo Editions, 1992.)

# Chapter 2

# <u>THE RACE TO IDENTIFY THE LETTER WRITER</u>

Subsequent letters in the book describe Jürnjakob's life in Iowa. As I read these letters, it seemed as though they were describing localities and events in the neighborhood where I grew up; the family names Brüning, Folgmann, Jahnke, Klüss, Krüger, Meier, Miller, Sass, Schneider, Schröder, Schuldt, Schmidt, Timmermann and Völss were all familiar to me. I found that at one time a town with the name Springfield had existed 7 miles from where I grew up (Figs. 2.1 and 2.2), and became convinced that at least one of the letter writers was from this part of Iowa. But alas, the name Swehn was not familiar to me and is not to be found in Iowa census records – at least not from 1870 through 1900. Following various leads, I examined the profiles of numerous other families in Clayton County, including that of my greatgrandfather Wilhelm Oldag. He was a farmer, lived close to the site which was at one time Springfield, and had a daughter Bertha and a son who graduated from the University of Iowa in 1907 and became a highly respected doctor. But none of these profiles matched Jürnjakob's.

Little by little, and over a period of many years, I learned that I was not the only person searching for Jürnjakob Swehn – and not the only person having difficulties in the search. In 1988 I mentioned my dilemma to two friends, Franz Schubert and Dr. Günther Schröder, in Göttingen, Germany who were avid genealogists with special interests in Mecklenburg. (I'm sad to say that both are now deceased.) They alerted me to literature [5, 7-9] addressing Swehn and the author of the book. This literature confirms that Swehn is a pseudonym but that, although many had tried, none had identified even one of the letter writers. Their input was a key to my progress in the race to be the first to establish Jürnjakob's true identity.

I learned much later that clues as to the identity of the primary letter writer had been published already in 1930. In his article, "Out of Johannes Gillhoff's last Year," H.K.A. Krüger, a friend of Gillhoff, quotes from conversations he had with Gillhoff [10]. According to Gillhoff, "A Wiedow, who I baptized Swehn, was the most enthusiastic letter writer. Wieschen, his wife, worked as a hired girl for us for many years. When

12

I got his letter in Parchim, the point at which he told of plowing in the woods, I told myself, this man has that which thousands of writers seek in vain, a unique style, clear and natural; his eyes are open, he can narrate, and he doesn't lose anything on the way from the brain to the paper. ___ It is however peculiar that none of the early critics, as already more than 50,000 copies have been sold, had discovered Jürnjakob's most important characteristic: in his entire life, he never lost his sense of wonder. That struck me immediately in the original letters. The critics talk always about the clarity of the representation, but don't notice that the center of the work lies in Jürnjakob's personality." When asked (in 1929) if Jürnjakob was still alive, Gillhoff replied, "No. He died in 1915. However, Wieschen is still alive, and lives with her son, the doctor. She still congratulated the Eldena Congregation on the occasion of the 700-year celebration (1929), and the greetings were read also from the pulpit."

In 1977, Werner Schnoor [8] wrote that also Otto Theeß, a former student of Gillhoff, was aware that Jürnjakob Swehn was really named Wiedow. Schnoor confirms that this Wiedow did work for a Timmermann; he writes that the Timmermann farm is on the road from Glaisin to Menkendorf but that in 1977 only remains of the house were to be seen; also that Gillhoff named him Swehn because it means swine herder and Swehn's father was a swine herder.

In 1986, Hartmut Brun [5], author of several books on Johannes Gillhoff and a recipient of the Johannes-Gillhoff Prize in 1990, also wrote that Johannes Gillhoff revealed shortly before his death that Swehn was indeed a Wiedow, and that he was from the same village as Gillhoff. The statements by Schnoor and Brun imply that, although more than one letter writer may have been involved, most of the material for the book came from a single source. Brun had searched for Jürnjakob's identity and had found the Auswanderungs-Consens (Permit to Emigrate) dated 1870 for Joachim Wiede, his wife Sophie and their two youngest children, Johann and Anna. Since this family did not fit Jürnjakob's profile, Brun looked further and suggested that Swehn was more likely Johann H.C. Jalaß, also from Glaisin. However, two years later, in his definitive work on Gillhoff [9], Brun did not address this question.

A copy of a letter from Walter Kamphoefner, a Professor at Texas A&M and a historian of immigration, to Hartmut Brun dated 10 January 1990 documents that Kamphoefner had cooperated with Brun in the late 1980's in the search for the identity of the primary letter writer. (Kamphoefner sent me a copy of the letter in 2000.) He had found, in the 1880 US Census, a family headed by a John Viedow living in Garnavillo Township, Clayton

County, Iowa. But this family also did not match Jürnjakob's profile. He had no idea how close he was to "cracking the case."

At the symposium on "Jürnjakob Swehn: Wahrheit und Legende (Truth and Legend)," held on Lake Müritz in Mecklenburg-Vorpommern in Spring 1993, Erhard Böttcher reported that he had travelled "far and wide in Iowa during the summer of 1992 in search of any trace ___ of descendants belonging to the real Swehn – but found absolutely none." [6] In a recent personal communication, Böttcher wrote that he didn't know that the name Swehn was a pseudonym.

In the summer of 1996, a 31-year-old graduate student at the Free University of Berlin, Kai Brauer by name, entered the race somewhat belatedly and briefly. Working on his doctorate degree in sociology, he was studying farm-family structures in the Mecklenburg region of Germany and in Iowa. Visiting Iowa in both 1996 and 1997, he became interested in determining whether Johannes Gillhoff's book was based on facts or whether, as believed by many, it was pure fiction. His first visit is reported in the 12 September 1996 issue of The Pioneer-Republican, his second visit in the 28 September 1997 issue of the Des Moines Sunday Register. He was particularly excited when finding the notation in the church books at Victor, Iowa confirming that the immigrant Johann Joachim Jalass had been killed by a train, as described in Gillhoff's book. Although he didn't identify the writer of the letters, his activities did motivate me to publish my findings somewhat earlier than I might have otherwise.

In the fall of 1996, Udo Baarck from Glaisin visited Iowa on the occasion of the 150th anniversary of statehood for Iowa. He brought with him a keen interest in emigration from Glaisin to Iowa and copies of old letters sent by the Fründt family in Victor, Iowa to relatives in Glaisin. In Victor, he met Valerie Hansen, a descendant of the Fründt family from Glaisin, and Bill Kuesel, a descendant of the Köhn family from Glaisin. At the St. John's Cemetery near Victor, he saw family names which matched many of the names in Gillhoff's book. A comparison of birthdates with those given in the Eldena church records confirmed that many of those buried at St. John's were indeed born in Glaisin. But he was not able to identify anyone as being Jürnjakob Swehn.

We see that the search for the identity of Jürnjakob Swehn had become a race – even though some of the participants were not aware of the activities of the others.

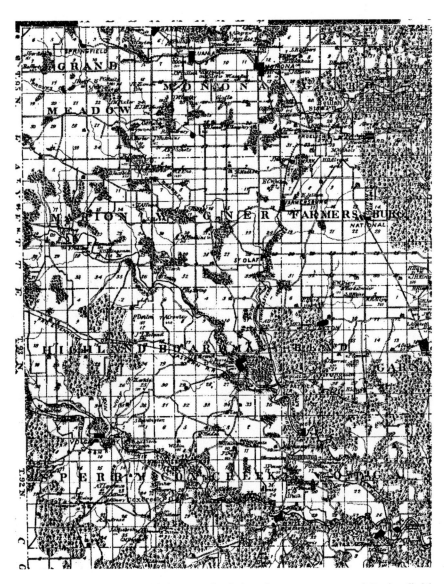

Fig. 2.1 The first map which I acquired showing a town named Springfield in Grand Meadow Township, Clayton County, Iowa. I grew up near Luana, seven miles east of Springfield. The map is from A.T. Andreas, Illustrated Historical Atlas of the State of Iowa. Chicago: Andreas Atlas Co., 1875.

Fig. 2.2 A street sign on the east side of Postville, Iowa, memorializing the now-extinct town of Springfield. (Photo by E.L. Knuth, 1998)

# Chapter 3

# SWEHN WAS INDEED A WIEDOW

Upon my return to California the last week of May 1988 I was filled with enthusiasm, eager to search for Wiedow families. The goal of this search was to find records of a Wiedow family which fit the profile of the Jürnjakob Swehn family found in the book. Characteristics of this family included immigration by Jürnjakob in 1868 at the age of 19 from Glaisin (in Mecklenburg) to Iowa, marriage to Wieschen Schröder (also from Glaisin), and at least three children. The oldest son, Heinrich, studied in Iowa City and Germany, became a doctor, had a wife named Cora and a son named Charly. Jürnjakob's youngest son, who eventually took over the farm, signed his letter in the book as Hans. A daughter, who was not yet married when Jürnjakob wrote his last letter, signed her letters as Berti.

In spite of the work which had accumulated (including 6 weeks of mail), I made time to go to the Family History Center – known better to many genealogists as "The Mormon Library." My starting point for the search was the US Census for Iowa. In the 1870 census (the first census after Jürnjakob's arrival in 1868) I found three entries in Clayton County with phonetic spellings of Wiedow – a John Veto with wife and two children, another John Veto with wife and twelve children, and a Henry Wedor, 15 years of age and born in Iowa. None matched the profile of Jürnjakob Swehn – a disappointment! But in the 1880 census, I found an individual in Clayton County who was not listed in 1870 – a Carl Wiedow with wife, Elisa, and three children – Henry, Mary and Elisa. He was a farmer, 32 years of age, born in Mecklenburg. Could this be Jürnjakob? Perhaps, but I needed more confirmation.

For 1890, we have for all practical purposes no census; nearly all of the records were destroyed in a very unfortunate sequence of events. First they were damaged in the fire on January 10, 1921 in the Commerce Building in Washington, D.C. – the severity of the damage being aggravated by storage of the 1890 census outside the vault. Then destruction of the damaged records was authorized, perhaps through a mistake, by Congress in December 1932. Although records for 6,160 persons are available today, none for Iowa.

I approached the 1900 census with anticipation and intrepidation. On the one hand, this census contains more information of interest to genealogists than does any other US census. On the other hand, what if Carl Wiedow were not to be found? I breathed a huge sigh of relief when I found in Iowa County a Chas. Wiedow with wife, Lizzie, and two children, Chas. and Bertha. (Fig. 3.1) He was a farmer, 52 years of age, born in Germany – obviously the same husband and wife as found in the 1880 census. The census indicated also that the husband was born in November 1847, Lizzie was born in September 1847, both were born in Germany, both immigrated in 1868, he was a naturalized citizen, they were married 27 years, she had given birth to five children, and all five children were still alive. Carl Wiedow's age, place of birth, year of immigration and daughter's name fit the Jürnjakob Swehn profile! This must be Jürnjakob!

This information provided excellent guidelines for further research, both in Mecklenburg and in Iowa. Combining the birth information from the census with references to the Eldena church (in Mecklenburg) in the book [1], I was able to find relatively quickly, from the film of the Eldena church books, the birth records for both Chas. and Lizzie. (Figs. 3.2-3.3) Chas. was born in Bellevue (near Eldena) on Nov. 8, 1847 and christened Carl Friederich Johann Julius Wiedow. Lizzie was born in Glaisin on Sept. 29, 1847 and christened Catharina Elizabeth Johanna Schröder. According to Clayton County civil records, Carl applied for citizenship on March 11, 1872 (Fig. 3.4); civil and church records document that he married Elisabeth Schröder five days later. (On p. 22 of the Jürnjakob Swehn book [2] we find that Jürnakob married Wieschen Schröder. I consider it likely that the pet name Wieschen was derived somehow from Lieschen, a pet name for Elisabeth.)

I noted from the 1900 census that the Wiedow family lived in Lincoln Township and, in October of 1988, ordered from the Family History Center (Mormon Library) the film for the Lincoln Township Church. (Fig. 3.5). The church was indeed St. John's, where Carl Wiedow's family went to church after they moved to Iowa County! 1988 was 12 years after I was made aware of Jürnjakob Swehn in 1976 and 8 years before Kai Brauer and Udo Baarck made their initial visits to Iowa in 1996.

Carl and Elisabeth had five children; Heinrich (Henry), Maria (Mame), Elisabeth Dorothea Marie (Lizzie), Karl Heinrich Wilhelm (Charly) and Bertha Caroline. The first three children were born and baptized in Clayton County, and appear with the parents in the 1880 census. The last two were born and baptized in Iowa County, and appear with the parents in the 1900 census. The oldest son, Henry, became a medical doctor (having studied both at the University of Iowa and at Berlin University) and married a neighbor's daughter, Cora Simpson. The second son, Charly, took over the farm. (On p. 174 of the book [2] is implied that Hans took over the farm. Apparently the youngest son was christianed Karl Heinrich Wilhelm, went by Hans during his youth, and used Charly as an adult. In going by Hans during his youth, he might have been deferring to his father, Carl, and his older brother, Heinrich.) Bertha married in November 1912; her father, Carl Wiedow, passed away in November 1913. (This is consistent with the last chapter of the book, in which Swehn writes that Berti is not yet married; it also implies that the last chapter was written at least a year before Swehn passed away.)

After identifying Carl Wiedow with Jürnjakob in 1988, I continued to research the Wiedow family calmly and with the feeling that no-one was breathing at my back. Brun apparently had arrived at a dead end [5] and I had no inkling that Kamphoefner had joined the search. I included in my researches the genealogies of Carl (alias Jürnjakob) and Elisabeth (alias Wieschen), visualizing that their Ahnentafels (family trees) would be substantial additions to an initial publication. As is frequently the case, the genealogy took more time than I had expected. And the possibility of descendants of Carl and Elisabeth still living in Iowa occurred to me. But since I had not yet connected to the internet, finding people was not as easy then as it would be today.

Then, in May 1993, a fortuitous window of opportunity opened. Fifty years had slipped by since graduation of our high-school class (Luana High School, Class of 1943). We scheduled a class reunion for the weekend of 8-9 May. On the way from the Cedar Rapids Airport to the Pines Motel in Postville, my wife and I stopped in Elkader to say Hello to our very dear friend, Myra Voss, President of the Clayton County Chapter of the Iowa Genealogical Society. She had been instrumental in 1986 in helping me to find my two half brothers (Gene Koevenig and Ron Huff), had invited me to speak at the Iowa Genealogical Society Seminar in 1987, and more recently had provided invaluable help in my search for Wiedow records in Clayton County. It didn't take very long for the conversation to drift to Carl Wiedow. When I expressed an interest in Carl's descendants, Myra volunteered to call a cousin, Oris Martens, who lived in Amana, i.e., in Iowa County. Both Myra and Oris are descendants of the Schult (Schultz) family from Glaisin – the Schult family which had settled in Iowa County and is noted for its large annual family reunions. In about two minutes we had the names of two living Wiedow descendants (Clark Wiedow and his sister Mrs. Alton Wolf) and the phone number of the Wolf residence – and my weekend was looking very promising!

Sunday, after attending church services at the Lutheran Church in Luana where most of my high-school class had been baptised and confirmed, Margaret and I returned briefly to the Pines Motel – mostly to phone the Wiedow descendants. (For me, the motel was largely utilitarian, the most exciting feature being the meadowlark which sang so cheerfully in a nearby field.) I dialed the Wolf residence, a lady answered and informed me rather promptly that, whatever it was I was selling, she didn't want any. After I assured her that I wasn't selling anything and explained how I had gotten her number, we confirmed that she was indeed born a Wiedow, had never heard of Jürnjakob Swehn, and had no idea that any letters her grandfather might have written had been published. Eventually we agreed to meet at her home late afternoon of the next day. She gave me directions to her home, a white house with a windmill on the property, and said she would invite her brother, Harold, and her daughter to join us.

The next morning, after breakfast in Ginger's coffee shop in Postville, we checked out of the Pines and headed towards Iowa County. The Amana Colonies were on the way to Iowa County, sounded like an interesting stopover, and might be the ideal place to spend the night. Driving through the familiar corn fields, I reflected back on the weekend and looked forward to the rest of the day. The weekend had been good. The reunion had been truly exceptional. After 50 years, all 18 members of the class were still alive, and 16 had participated in the reunion. It must have been a combination of good genes and good luck! My visit to the Postville Public Library had been rewarding. I had found my greatgrandmother's obituary (full of useful details) in a 1918 edition of the Postville Herald. And Elaine Ball, my favorite dancing partner from my high-school days, had made the effort to catch up with me there. Hopefully the rest of the day would be as good as the weekend had been. After all, it was my birthday!

In Amana, we checked out the "Bed and Breakfasts" and decided that the Noe Haus was the ideal place to spend the night. It was one of the older buildings in the town, unusually well built and with turn-of-the-century decor. We had lunch at the Brick Haus Restaurant. The menu included the traditional Wiener Schnitzel (veal cutlet), Kassler Ripschen (smoked pork chops) and Bratwurst. Several members of the older generation in the restaurant can still handle German, although it came through with a noticeable dialect, known locally as Kolonie Deutsch. (The first settlers in Amana emigrated from southwest Germany in 1842 and settled in Amana in 1852.) After visiting several of the craftshops, we headed for Iowa County and our appointment with the Wiedows. Highway 151, through the Amana Colonies, was interesting. But Highway 80, with its long straight stretches and speeding trucks, was monotonous. After turning off on Victor Road, I stopped to check my notes regarding directions. But my briefcase with my notes, Wiedow files and the Jürnjakob Swehn book was not in the car! I had left it at the Bed and Breakfast! To go back to Amana and come back would take most of two hours; I had to do as best I could with my memory. The most awkward part was showing up without the highly-touted book.

Even though we arrived empty handed, we were greeted warmly. Present were Harold and Elsie Wiedow, Alton and Alice Wolf, and Sharon McKay, daughter of Alice Wolf. Harold and Alice, son and daughter of Charly Wiedow, lived not far from the farm on which Carl and Elisabeth had raised their family. The first visit with them was an emotional evening. They had never heard of the book, and could hardly believe that letters written by their grandfather had become so famous. For me, the search for Jürnjakob Swehn, which had its beginnings in 1976 in Schwerin, had reached a high point. We compared the book with their memories, frequently with agreement. They brought out old photos of the family, including a priceless photo of Carl, Elisabeth and their five children (Figs. 3.6-3.7). Henry's gold watch, mentioned on p. 47 of the book [2], is still in the family. Henry received it when he graduated from high school. Since it is engraved HW, it has been passed down via family members with the same initials. We drove around the neighborhood. The barn on the old Wiedow farm still stood at that time (Fig. 3.8) but has been dismantled since then; the house had been replaced. Lincoln Township Schoolhouse No. 4, where Carl and Elisabeth's two youngest children went to school, still stood (Fig. 3.9) although not in use; the original church schoolhouse has been replaced. The St. John's Lutheran church, built in 1895, is still in use, but the steeple was replaced by a shorter steeple after it was toppled by a windstorm in 1950. (Figs. 3.10-3.12) Carl, Elisabeth, Carl's father (Jochim) and Elisabeth's mother (Maria Rösch) are buried in the church cemetery; Elisabeth's father (Johann) is buried in Garnavillo, Iowa. The gravestone of Carl and Elisabeth is impressive. (Fig. 3.13) In two cases, the book contained information which the family members could not corroborate that evening. They did not know that Heinrich and Cora had a son; a subsequent search of family letters confirmed that they had a son and that he had passed away at an early age. They also did not remember the south side of the old house in sufficient detail to corroborate the description given on p. 25 of the book [2]; a subsequent search of family photos uncovered several photos of the house which fits Swehn's description, including his description of the large window on the south side of the house. (Figs. 3.14-3.15) As we were getting ready to leave, Alice invited us to view more of the house. The living room reminded me of the living rooms I had known in Clayton County as a child – well furnished

21

and used mainly to entertain visitors. I was impressed by Alice's display of doll-head vases. As we reluctantly parted company at the end of this memorable evening, Alice presented Margaret with a copy of the Deep River Community Cookbook which included not only favorite recipes from the Wiedow family but also early community photos. Sharon and I agreed that she would stop at our Bed and Breakfast on her way back to her home (in Cedar Rapids) and pick up the Jürnjakob Swehn book and the Wiedow family sheets which I had put together. A life-long relationship had been cemented.

In 1996 I visited Bertha Wiedow's grandson, who is living in the house in Muscatine, Iowa in which Bertha and her family had lived. It is noted with interest that Berti describes a visit to Muscatine on p. 67 of the book [2].

Subsequently I made contact with both the son-in-law and the grandson of Henry. The son-in-law is the widower of the adopted daughter of Henry and Cora. (The mother of this girl died at her birth in the hospital where Henry was practicing.) The family still has a grandfather's clock which Henry and Cora brought back from Germany.

The association of Carl Wiedow with Jürnjakob Swehn is brought into focus in the following table.

### COMPARISON OF SWEHN AND WIEDOW FAMILIES

| SWEHN | WIEDOW |
|---|---|
| Immigrated in 1868, at age 19 | Immigrated in 1868, at age 20 |
| Married Wieschen Schröder | Married Elisabeth Schröder |
| Oldest son Heinrich Doctor, studied in Iowa City & Germany Wife Cora Son Charly | Oldest son Henry Doctor, studied in Iowa City, Vienna & Berlin Wife Cora Simpson Son |
| Son Hans took over farm | Son Charly took over farm |
| Daughter Berti | Daughters Maria, |

## Lizzie & Bertha

We see that Swehn was indeed a Wiedow!

We also see now why Brun [4] failed to associate Wiedow with Swehn. He found, in Germany, emigration records for Carl Wiedow's parents, brother and sister, but none for Carl. Apparently Carl emigrated without going through the formality of applying for a consent to emigrate! Hence, Brun's findings did not match Swehn's profile.

Why Prof. Kamphoefner didn't find a Wiedow which matched Jürnjakob is also now understandable. He focused on Garnavillo and Farmersburg Townships in Clayton County, the new-world home of many of the immigrants from the Eldena Congregation. In the 1880 census, he found in Garnavillo Township a family headed by a John Viedow who did not match Jürnjakob's profile, but didn't find in the neighboring Read Township the family headed by Carl Wiedow.

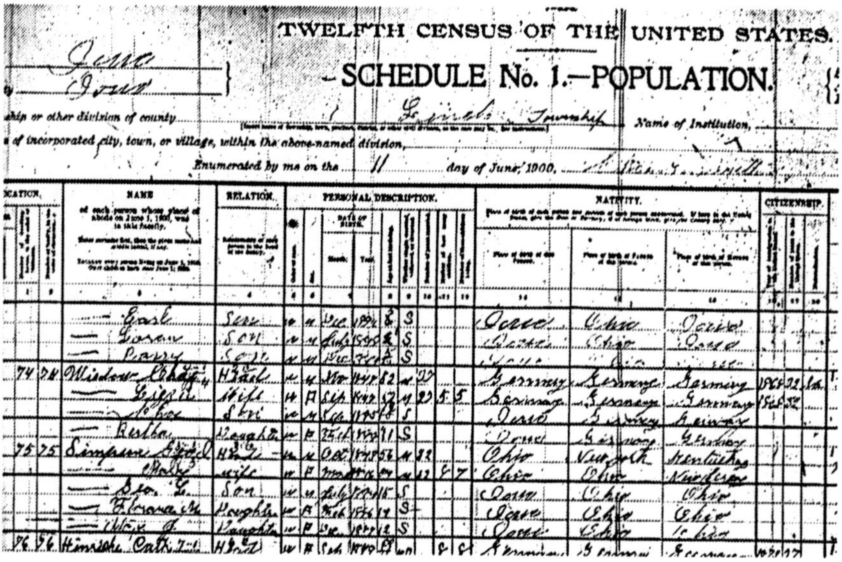
TWELFTH CENSUS OF THE UNITED STATES.

SCHEDULE No. 1.—POPULATION.

Fig. 3.1 Page from the 1900 US Census, Lincoln Township, Iowa County, Iowa showing Chas. and Lizzie Wiedow with children Chas. and Bertha.

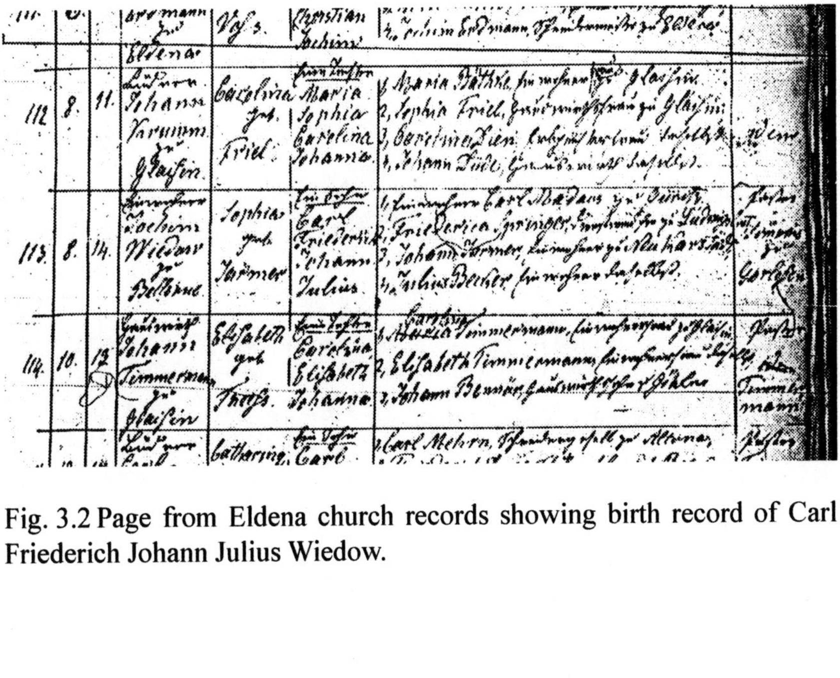

Fig. 3.2 Page from Eldena church records showing birth record of Carl Friederich Johann Julius Wiedow.

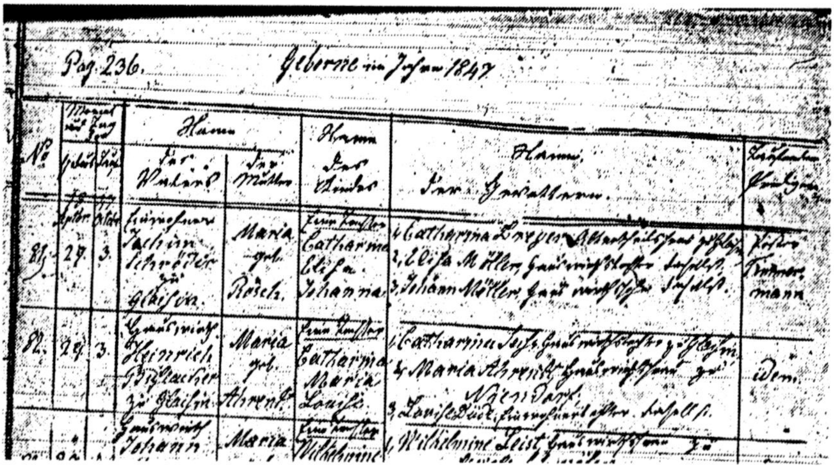

Fig. 3.3 Page from Eldena church records showing birth record of Catharina Elisa Johanna Schröder.

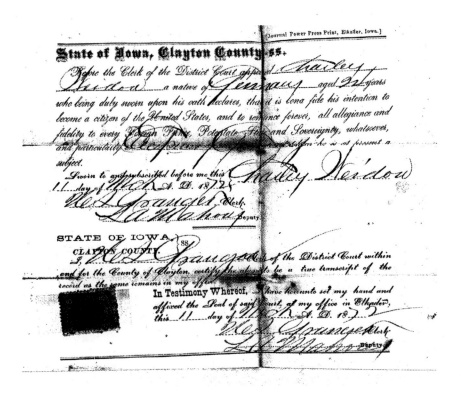

Fig. 3.4 Application for citizenship, Charley Weidow. Variations in the spelling of the Wiedow family name were common.

**Microfilm Order—Family History Center**

| | | |
|---|---|---|
| (12) Family History Center name | | (13) Family History Center number |

| | | |
|---|---|---|
| PATRON: Please TYPE or PRINT items 1 through 9. For example of microfilm numbers, see reverse side. | (8) Loaned to (check one)<br>☐ LDS member<br>☒ Non-member | (14) Order number<br>**69607** |
| (1) Single number microfilm order    1 0 0 3 4 2 8 | (9) Type of loan (check one)   Charges<br>☒ Three-weeks   $ 2 50<br>☐ Six-months<br>☐ Indefinite | (15) If changed to six-months or indefinite give original order number |
| (2) Multiple number microfilm order      thru | | |
| (3) Title of record    *Lincoln Twp Church*    Item number | | |
| (4) Patron's name   *E Knuth*    (5) Telephone number *(818)344-1533* | ☐ Change to six-months<br>☐ Change to indefinite | (16) Director *K. Inselmann* |
| (6) Street address   *18085 Boris Dr.* | (10) Postage    $ .25 | (17) Date ordered *18/10/88* |
| (7) City, state or country, and zip code   *Encino CA 91316* | (11)   $<br>Amount collected   2.75 | (18) Due date |
| | PINK—Patron's Copy | PFGS0142 6/88 Printed in USA |

Fig. 3.5 The order form, dated 18 October 1988, for the film corresponding to the Lincoln Township Church, Iowa County, Iowa.

Fig. 3.6 The Wiedow family in about 1895. Front row: Carl, Bertha and Elisabeth. Back row: Lizzie, Henry, Charly and Mame. (Photo courtesy of Harold Wiedow)

Fig. 3.7 A Wiedow family photo (from about 1907) which includes Carl's pipe -- about which Berti complains on page 67 of the book [2]. Behind Carl are Bertha and Mame; the man on the far right is Cary Sheppard. The three children, from left to right, are Margaret, Bernice and Harriet Sheppard, children of Cary and Mame. (Photo courtesy of Harold Wiedow)

Fig. 3.8 The barn on the Wiedow farm.(Photo by E.L. Knuth, 1993)

Fig. 3.9 Lincoln Township School No. 4, where Carl and Elisabeth's two youngest children went to school. Left to right: Julie Wolf, Alice (Wiedow) Wolf and Alton Wolf. (Photo courtesy of Alice Wolf)

Fig. 3.10 St. John's Lutheran Church, Victor, Iowa. (Photo by E.L. Knuth, 1993)

Fig. 3.11 St. John's Lutheran Church, Victor, Iowa as it appeared before the wind storm of May 5, 1950.

Alice (Wiedow) Wolf

Fig. 3.12 ~~Elsie (nee Prashak)~~ and Harold Wiedow at St. John's Lutheran Church; they kindly provided me with a guided tour of the Wiedow neighborhood. (Photo by E.L. Knuth, 1993)

Fig. 3.13  Gravestone of Carl Wiedow and Elisabeth Schröder (AKA Jürnjakob and Wieschen), St. John's Lutheran Cemetery, Victor, Iowa. (Photo by E.L. Knuth, 1993)

Fig. 3.14 The Wiedow house, described on page 25 of the book [2]. (Photo courtesy of Adena Sheppard)

Fig. 3.15 The Wiedow house in wintertime. The photo was taken by Charly Wiedow in about 1910; the note was written by his wife, Velda (Forney) Wiedow. (Photo courtesy of Sharon McKay)

# Chapter 4

# LETTERS FROM THE OLD SCHOOLTEACHER

The preceding chapters have referenced literature and reviewed evidence which establishes that Carl Wiedow was "the most enthusiastic letter writer" among those whose letters were included in the book and attributed to Jürnjakob Swehn. It would be most interesting to read letters which Gottlieb Gillhoff, the old schoolteacher in the Mecklenburg village of Glaisin, wrote in turn to Carl Wiedow. Unfortunately, no letter from Gillhoff addressed to the Wiedow family has been found. However, two letters written by the schoolteacher to a neighboring Rösch family have survived. Carolina (nee Schütt) Rösch was a cousin of Gottlieb Gillhoff; Carolina's father and Gottlieb's mother were siblings. Also, Carolina's husband, Johann Rösch, was an uncle of Elisabeth (nee Schröder) Wiedow, the Wieschen in the book; Johann and Elisabeth's mother were siblings. (See Appendix A.) These letters provide direct evidence of correspondence between Gottlieb Gillhoff and the Wiedow family when Gillhoff writes, "That my dear wife died more than two years ago you have probably heard already from Wiedow." I have translated these letters and include them here in their entirety in order to provide the reader with insight into the character and roles of the old schoolteacher. Copies of these letters were provided the present author by descendants of the Rösch family, namely by Larry Rösch of Iowa City, Iowa.

Glaisin/Eldena

28 February 1890

To all you dear ones!

Dear cousin, I was very pleased to receive your letter. From this letter I see that the God Almighty has brought you trials this past year. In the deaths of your dear children and in the illness of your dear daughter Maria, who I knew as a small child, I hope you had consolation and relief from the prayers to him, who calls all those suffering and burdened to him, so that he can comfort them. Just as a shepherd, when his sheep don't want to go into the barn, first puts a lamb in the barn, which the sheep then soon follow, so does our God Almighty sometimes take the children, so that the parents and the remaining family develop a desire and longing for heaven. For those who love God, all things work out for the best. So bear up under the trials imposed by your God without complaining and strive above all such that you and your loved ones reach that goal of faith, the salvation of your souls. *(Note by author: The children mentioned here must be Heinrich, who died 8 March 1889, Caroline, who died 26 Aug. 1889, and Maria, who was born in Glaisin 9 August 1864.)* – So far the dear God has granted me and my family good health. In June, our Fritz became the father of a baby girl, who was named Magdalene, as is her mother. Our fifth son, Gustav, also went to Schwaan as a teacher, lives with his brother and eats at his table. The youngest son Theodor was transferred last fall from Göhlen to Leussow and will enter the Seminary next fall if he passes his exams. The other three sons are still at their old positions. None of them is engaged or married yet, although Gottlieb is now already 30. *(Note by author: The Gillhoff's had seven children, born in the odd-numbered years from 1857 through 1869.)* My dear wife, thank God, is still always healthy enough so that, together with her sister Line, they can handle the household. She is also already in her 56th year, while I entered my 58th in the fall. – The past summer brought us only a very meager harvest of rye and oats, but the potato harvest turned out good. We also got enough feed for the cattle. Rye costs 8½ Marks for 100#, oats 8 Marks. Pigs cost 40 to 45 M per 100#, calves 36 to 40 M. Shortly before Christmas we got 100 M for a calf which weighed 262#. – Local resident Johann Saß passed away this past summer. This winter, Johann Henning, the aged Johann Meier and Penzholz's wife passed away. Just before Christmas, a three-year old daughter of the hereditary tenant Theeß came too close to the fire in the kitchen and burned herself so severely that she had to be taken to Bethlehem, where she died several days later. *(Note by author: Bethlehem is a hospital in the nearby city of Ludwigslust.)* I must write also something about my sisters. Luisa is quite ill and will not be with us much longer. *(Note by author: Luisa is obviously the older sister, baptized Louise Amalia Maria and born 16 September 1834.)* She has a bad case of asthma. The doctor examined her and found that her heart is twice as large as it should be. She is awaiting her end with patience and resignation, now wishing only that the Lord would take her mercifully. Her son is a helper in a bookstore in Leipzig, with an annual salary of 1800 M. Mina likes it in Neuwied and has so much work sewing that she hardly can keep up. *(Note by author: Mina must be the younger sister, baptized Catharina Wilhelmina Lucia and born 4 May 1838.)* – Wheelwright Fründt and his wife celebrated their Golden Wedding Anniversary on the 25th of February. They received 50 Marks from the Grand Duke and 25 Marks from the village.

Now I wish for you, dear Mother Rösch, and for you, dear Cousin, and for all of your loved ones, the grace of God. On this earth we will not see each other again; each of us will have to struggle and take care so that we will all be among those to whom the Lord will say: Come to me, you who are blessed by my father, inherit the kingdom that has been prepared for you from the beginning of the earth. May God grant this!

We have had quite a mild winter. It was frost weather for almost all of February, the windows didn't freeze even once. Yesterday a little snow fell.

My wife and sister-in-law send the best of greetings, also Jochim Dien and wife, who are quite well. Greet all who I know in your neighborhood.

Hearty greetings from your cousin

G. Gillhoff

Glaisin

22 Aug. 1907

Dear Cousin,

I was really pleased from the heart to get a letter from you, and in it also a photo of your son, who has unquestionably a resemblance around the eyes to your brother Christian. *(Note by author: The son mentioned here must be Louis, 1872-1924, the only son alive at the time this letter was written.)* How kind of our dear God, that he has once again provided you with this son! Ja, with each sorrow we have nevertheless also much for which to be thankful, dear cousin, and, when we blissfully have prevailed, must praise God for having made all well. *(Note by author: The sorrows to which Gillhoff refers here might be the untimely deaths of four children, Caroline, 1869-1889, Heinrich, 1878-1889, Maria, 1864-1904, and Elisabeth, 1867-1904.)*

It pleases me immensely, that you consider it better to work than to be lazy. I agree, and therefore I've not been able to convince

41

myself to give up my position. I'm thinking to stay here until next Easter and then go to live with my youngest son Theodor, who is supervisor at the rescue mission in Gehlsdorf near Rostock. But I should not count on many more years since I will be 75 years old in the fall. However, I am still quite sturdy, only that I am short of breath so that I can no longer do much physical work. I have now 11 grandchildren. My oldest son Fritz lives in Bremen and is a missionary to the emigrants. Recently I visited him for 8 days, and we enjoyed our time together very much. He has a very lovely wife and 2 children. The daughter is 17, the son 14 years of age. The son was confirmed at Eastertime.

The widow of my deceased son Gottlieb lives in Ludwigslust, where both of her daughters are going to school; the son is with Fritz in Bremen. My son Johannes is a seminary teacher in Prussia and is not married. Also the next son Karl is not married, was at first a teacher in Dömitz, and transferred then to Niendorf near Dömitz, from where he visits me regularly. Gustav is a teacher in Schwaan and has 4 children, and Theodor, of whom I have already written, has 2 sons. That my dear wife passed away more than two years ago you perhaps have heard already from Wiedow.

Now I'll answer your questions. My sister Mina is dead already 13 years, Luise already 15 years. The roofer Möller passed away this spring, his wife last year. He was blind in his last years. Johann Brüning is also dead already several years. He lived in great poverty. His wife moved this summer with her oldest son to Grabow, where her other two children also live. I often had felt quite sorry for the old man. In his later days he had to work much and hard, and became very bent-over. But the oldest son could see all this very calmly, and kept his hands in his pockets when his father was working hard. Jochim Dien and his wife retired several years ago. Both of them are quite crippled; they suffer a lot from rheumatism. Both of them send hearty greetings. Jürgen Röseler's widow is also dead almost 2 years. You, dear cousin, would not know many people here any more; ja, the whole village would seem strange to you. This summer, the 51st cottage will be built. Several weeks ago, we took also the old Mrs. Jauert to her grave.

You write about the rainy weather. Here it has been quite cold and also rainy all summer, so that one hardly had a true summer. Some loads of hay were brought in half dry. The weather was bad during all of the rye harvest, and also some loads of rye were brought in wet. However, the straw grew quite well. Also the oats grew well. Up to now, the dear God has protected us from hail, while in other parts of Mecklenburg much of the grain was hailed down.

As I see from my book, you, dear Cousin, are completing your 69th year on the 31st of October. I wish now for you God's blessings for your birthday. When emigrating, you took with you three daughters to America: Wilhelmine, Marie and Elisabeth. Now, when you write to me again, I would like to know which of these are still alive. God bless you, your children and your children's children. They certainly all wish to have their old grandmother here for still a long time. Now may God's will be done. He wants to teach us now all to strive for that which is over there. Our cousins from Kummer, Graak's daughters, have all passed away. The youngest, Marie, died this spring, almost 80 years of age. Finally, I would ask you to greet heartily for me all of your children, especially your son. Many thanks for the enclosed photos and I send you a photo of my sister Mina. At this time I don't have at hand one of myself. Now God bless you all! Salvation! That is to be our lot here below until we are permitted to go to our master of gladness.

Yesterday I showed Mrs. Diehn the photo of your son. She had hardly glanced at it when whe cried out: that's little Fritz!

Greetings to all the dear ones from Glaisin in your neighborhood and to you including your son and your daughters from your cousin

Gottl. Gillhoff

*(Note by author: We see that, among the roles of the schoolteacher, was the important role of communicator between those left behind in Glaisin and those who had emigrated. He frequently read the letters from America to a group of villagers and then later penned responses according to the wishes of the villagers.)*

# Chapter 5

# LETTERS FROM THE TEACHER'S YOUNGEST SON

I found even more interesting three letters from the old school teacher's youngest son, Theodor Gillhoff (1869-1959). Theodor had emigrated to America and taken a position as teacher in Holyoke, Massachusetts. The first letter is addressed to the Pastor in Victor, Iowa, where Carl Wiedow and family went to church. The other two letters are addressed to the Jahlas family. The main thrust of the letter to the Pastor was to inquire if the Wiedow who wrote the letters was still alive. The publication three years earlier of the book which was based at least in part on these letters was not mentioned. Nevertheless, Theodor's letter confirms that the correspondence between Carl Wiedow and his teacher was special. Copies of these letters were provided the present author by descendants of the Jahlas family, namely by Bill and Ruth Jahlas of Deep River, Iowa.

62 Franklin St.
Holyoke, Mass.,
Nov. 3, 1920

Pastor Wm. F. Ullerich,
Box 248,
Victor, Iowa

Dear Pastor!

Kindly allow me to take a moment of your time for correspondence! - My father, who passed away several years ago and was a teacher in Mecklenburg, Germany, was for many years in correspondence with a Wiedow in Victor, Iowa. This Wiedow emigrated as a young man to America. A long-time faithful devotion to my father, who was his teacher, and great love for his home village, Glaisin, which he had left behind, is expressed in his letters, and my father was drawn to him in genuine friendship.

About fifteen years ago, Wiedow's oldest son, a doctor, visited Germany and took advantage of the opportunity to visit also my father.

Now the passing of my dear father has ended this exchange of letters. However, we, my brothers in Germany and I here, all teachers as was my father, would very much like to know, if the elderly Wiedow is still alive. He was our father's friend and for this reason important to us. Through his letters, which attest to his honest character and his sincere christianity, and which, even when in earnest, still always were full of simple golden humor, he has become ever more dear, so that we would not like to lose track of him. Hence I would be much obliged if you would write if the above-named, who must be now in his seventies, is still alive, and if so, what his address is. My brothers wrote some time ago that he must have moved from Victor.

Thanking you sincerely in advance for your trouble, I remain respectfully your

Theo. Gillhoff

*Notes by author: A sequal to the Jürnjakob Swehn book [1] was started already prior to the death of Johannes Gillhoff in 1930; it was completed by Theodor Gillhoff and published in 1957 under the title "Möne Markow, der neue Amerikafahrer." [11] The author notes that, although the first book was published in 1917 and Theodor wrote the above letter in 1920, Theodor mentions neither the first book nor any possible plans for a second book. The Wiedow family did not learn of the books until the author informed them in 1993.*

62 Franklin St.
Holyoke, Mass.
Jan. 10, 1923

Dear Friend!

We received your letter and photo and were very pleased with both. Yes, in my opinion, that is clearly the face of a daughter! We also have had photos made recently and sent to Germany; one is extra – we send it to you. Since you had not written for so long, we thought already that you had completely forgotten us; now we are all the more pleased and know that you still think about us. We know also that you don't have much time to write in the summer and fall. We wish you once again a happy new year, although it is now really already late for that; but I think that one always accepts a good wish, and therefore we wish you a very happy and blessed New Year! May God the father give you and us all that we need for body and soul in this life and in the life hereafter!

We have received many letters from Germany recently. It appears to be bad there. The French don't leave them alone and demand so much that the Germans, even if they were twice as diligent, couldn't supply them, as much as they would like to. In addition, they take away one piece of land after the other. The German Mark has practically no value anymore. Before the war, my brother Johannes had a salary of 5,000 Marks per year. He wrote recently that he gets now almost a million Marks per year, nothing but scrip money. He says that, if he buys something, he almost needs a handcart to transport all the scrip money needed to pay for it; but what he can buy with that is so little that he can take it home in his vest pocket. I have asked my brother several times if I should send him a few dollars, but they wrote that it is not necessary – they can make it through; if I want to give something, I should give it to others who are worse off than they are. Then I did that, have also collected in my school and in the Ladies Society of our congregation and sent altogether $140 to the fund for children and old folks. A pastor from Berlin wrote to me recently, a 78-year-old lady came to him and begged for help. She lived in a miserable basement hole and looked hardly like a human being. For the last several weeks she had cooked potato skins, salted them and eaten the broth. That was her only nourishment. So it is for thousands of old people. They can't buy potatoes anymore. In Berlin, a single average-size potato costs 1-1/2 Marks. – My brother in Eldena wrote that the old Jauert in Glaisin, who Mother Jahlas certainly still knows, is still alive and still very active. He must be now very old.

You write that your handwriting is so poor. I don't find it so. But if you would sooner write in English and if writing in English is easier for you, then do it; I can read and understand it easily. Also let me know whether you would prefer me to use German or English script; for me it is all the same.

We are pleased that you had a good harvest. Yes, we would like to visit you sometime and see all of your doings and above all see you and talk with you and exchange a good mouthful of Plattdeutsch (low German) with Mother Jahlas and Mother Wiedow. It is very friendly of you to invite us to visit you sometime. If only the trip were not so far and didn't cost so much! Now we must save seriously, because our oldest son is at the teachers college and the youngest goes there also next fall. I have a great longing once again to be among people from our homeland. Several years ago I was at a Synodal meeting in Kingston in New York City. More than half of the people belonging to the congregation were from Mecklenburg, and I was happy to see them and they were happy to see me. But I was the only one there from Glaisin and surroundings. Yes, our dear old Glaisin! Isn't that so, Mother Jahlas, we won't forget, as old as we might get!

Now we send you many hearty greetings, and please greet also the Wiedow and Fruendt families.

Your friend,<br>Theodor Gillhoff

*Notes by author: The brother Johannes mentioned here is Johannes Gillhoff (1861-1930), author of the Jürnjakob Swehn book [1]. Mother Jahlas must be Dorathea (Schlichting) Jahlas (1854-1939), widow of the John Jahlas (1850-1895), who was killed in the unfortunate train accident near Deep River. Mother Wiedow must be Elisabeth (Schroeder) Wiedow (1847-1930), widow of Carl Wiedow (1847-1913); he wrote many of the letters used in the above book.*

62 Franklin St.<br>Holyoke, Mass.<br>Dec. 31, 1924

Dear Friends!

To be sure, I am very busy these days; however, I don't want to let the old year slip by without at least writing a short letter and thanking you for your letter and for your photo. We enjoyed them very much. But I would not have recognized Mother (Jahlas). I believe that I could have gone by her 10 times on the street without knowing who it was.

Many thanks also for the good wishes for Christmas and the New Year, and we wish also for you that God the Lord will grant you a happy, healthy and blessed New Year. We pray that he will do with you and with us as we find in the hymnal: "Give your kind blessings to all our paths; let the friendly sun shine on the great and on the small." We were especially pleased to hear from you since we already thought that you had forgotten about us, because you hadn't written for so long.

A difficult time is now behind us. Our oldest son was ill in September, just at the time that he was to start in a good position as principal of a public school. He had studied <u>too</u> hard, more than his nervous system could handle. Now he is living with us, and the doctor says that he shouldn't return to teaching until next fall. The youngest son is still studying, but was also with us for a week at Christmas.

We get news from Germany quite often. My brother Johannes lives now in Ludwigslust and gets to Glaisin often. Recently he visited also the old Jauert again. He is now 87 years old and still quite hale and hearty for his age. My brother publishes a paper called "Mecklenburgische Monatsschrift" (Mecklenburg Monthly). It costs one Mark per month. It contains stories and such things from Mecklenburg, also many pictures. We also want to get it.

With that I will close. But one thing I must nevertheless still tell. The teacher in Glaisin, who is there now in Father's position, doesn't believe in anything and doesn't hold classes in Catechism and Bible Stories. The mayor in Glaisin is now the young Düde, across from the Förster (restaurant). He came recently to my brother in Ludwigslust and related that the teacher in Glaisin had the students write an essay, and one of the older girls wrote: "I really don't like to be in school any more. At the beginning of the school day, we don't sing and pray any more, and also not at the end of the school day. It is just as though a herd of cattle is let in and out. With the old teacher it was entirely different." Then the new teacher became very red in the face.

With hearty greetings for you all and for Mother Jahlas

Theodor Gillhoff

# Chapter 6

# THEY DID SETTLE IN CLAYTON COUNTY

We see now that, among those who congregated in New York and then travelled to Iowa, the Schröder family is of particular interest. According to the passenger list, Johann and Dora Schröder (ages 58 and 45) and their daughter Elise (age 21) left Hamburg aboard the steamship Germania on Sept. 30 and arrived at New York on Oct. 15, i.e., about a month after Swehn. Eldena church records indicate that all three were born in Glaisin. (Also arriving on the Germania were Heinrich and Elise Schultz and their five children, also from Glaisin.) The timing is such that Johann is probably the Schröder who loaned Swehn the money for the trip to Iowa; Elise later became Carl Wiedow's wife. Incidentally, the grandchildren of the Wiedow-Schröder family recall independently, from family history handed down orally, that Grossvater came to America by sailship whereas Grossmutter came by steamship.

For Swehn and his friends, the anxiety of emigrating to a new land was lessened by the knowledge that they would be welcomed by relatives and friends. The emigration from the Eldena church congregation to Clayton County, Iowa had been in full swing for more than a decade. For example, passenger lists indicate that another group from Glaisin arrived earlier that year, on 21 May, aboard the steamship Saxonia from Hamburg. In the group were Johann and Dora Schröder's two oldest daughters Marie and Mina, Dora Schröder's youngest brother Johann Rösch and family, Johann Schultz' widow and four children, and a Heinrich Timmermann. They all settled in Clayton County.

We find indeed that Carl and Elisabeth Wiedow did live approximately 13 years in the community where my family had settled. They were married in Garnavillo in 1872; their first two children were baptized (1873 and 1874) in Garnavillo, the third child in Clayton Center (1879). See Figs. 6.1 and 6.2. These findings confirmed the feelings generated as I read the book for the first time. My greatgrandparents Garms were married in Garnavillo in 1856; Grossmutter Knuth (nee Garms) and my father were baptized in Clayton Center in 1866 and 1886. Swehn wrote that he and

49

Wieschen first rented a farm. Apparently they rented as long as they lived in Clayton County. The last record which I have found of them in Clayton County is from June 1880.

According to Brun [5], Carl Wiedow's parents, brother Johann and sister Maria emigrated in 1870. They are enumerated already in the 1870 U.S. Census, and were living in Garnavillo Township, Clayton County. (It is noted with interest that Carl is not to be found in the 1870 U.S. Census. According to his grandchildren, he left Germany without permission. This is consistent with our inability to find a consent-to-emigrate record. Did he therefore somehow avoid the census?) Carl's brother Johann married Wilhelmine Müller in 1875; they and their daughter Wilhelmine are enumerated in the 1880 U.S. Census, and were living in Grand Meadow Township, Clayton County, either in or near the town of Springfield. Carl's sister Maria married Heinrich Schrank in 1873 and apparently settled in Giard Township, Clayton County. Carl's father Jochim passed away in Iowa County in 1888. In spite of several searches, no record has been found of Carl's mother after 1874.

The village of Springfield is mentioned four times in the Jürnjakob Swehn book. I am aware of the Springfield which existed at one time in Grand Meadow Township in Clayton County; it was platted in 1869, but has been extinct now for many years. Kai Brauer, graduate student at the Free University of Berlin, found records of a Springfield in Keokuk County, immediately south of Iowa County. If a town with the name Springfield is relevant, the available information points to the one in Clayton County. Carl Wiedow's brother lived either in or near the Springfield in Clayton County; I have found no record of a Wiedow living in Keokuk County. The first mention of Springfield in the book, in Swehn's marriage proposal to Wieschen on p. 22 [2], has a ring of plausibility to it; many immigrants from the Eldena area settled first in central Clayton County and moved later to the northern part of the county. The other three mentions of it (a store selling pianos, a railroad station and a newspaper) might have been inserted by Gillhoff to provide continuity to the book. Incidentally, Springfield is today the second most frequent town name in the United States – second only to Fairview.

Also Elisabeth Schröder's family settled in Clayton County. The 1870 U.S. Census shows her brother, John, living with his parents in Volga Township and her second sister, Wilhelmine, married to Johann Heinrich Schultz, living in Garnavillo Township. Church records place her oldest sister, Maria, married to Karl Arend, near Garnavillo. Further details regarding the parents and siblings of Carl Wiedow and Elisabeth Schröder are given in Chapter 12.

The pattern of immigrants from the Eldena Congregation settling near other immigrants from the Eldena Congregation was repeated so often that, even today, the telephone directory for the Garnavillo area reads much like that for the Eldena area. The town of Garnavillo acquired its name in 1846, when the town name was changed from Jacksonville to Garnavillo. If the name change had occurred several decades later, the name New Eldena might have been a viable candidate!

Fig. 6.1 St. Paul's Lutheran Church, Garnavillo, Iowa. This building replaced that which burned in November 1878. (Photo by E.L. Knuth, 1993)

Fig. 6.2 Zion Lutheran Church, Clayton Center, Iowa. Dedicated in 1874. Perhaps the destruction of the Garnavillo church by fire in 1878 led to the baptism of the third Wiedow child (1879) being held at the neighboring church in Clayton Center. (Photo coutesty of Diane Breitsprecher)

# Chapter 7

# ON HIS OWN FARM

According to Carl Wiedow's obituary, the family moved to Iowa County in 1881. This year is consistent with the U.S. Census records, indicating that they were in Clayton County in June 1880, and the first dated entry involving Carl and Elisabeth in church records in Iowa County, indicating that they were in Iowa County in July 1881. If they conformed to Iowa-farmer tradition, they probably moved in about March of 1881. In Iowa County, they bought their own land. Jürnjakob describes the fulfillment of his "American Dream" in the chapter titled "On my own Farm." He writes that hard work was required to clear the land, one must have iron in the blood, and it costs much sweat. He writes also that, in order to succeed in America, one needs to be much more aggressive than in Germany and (perhaps a little regretfully) one has less time to be friendly. A farmer had to be many things – carpenter, cabinet maker, wagonmaker, blacksmith, mason and shoemaker. The adjustment was more difficult for the older people than for the younger ones. He describes in detail and with pride their farm – the land, buildings, animals, machinery, crops, prices, etc. He was especially proud of their house. It had eight rooms with solid walls, decorated with colorful wallpaper, and large windows. He was particularly pleased with the window on the south side, a 3-ft by 5-ft pane surrounded by smaller colored panes, and the large veranda. The grandchildren remember the wallpaper, which is documented also in Fig. 3.6. The house was indeed a dramatic improvement over the family cottage in Glaisin.

In 2002, Dr. Dieter Rakow, recipient of the Johannes Gillhoff Prize in 1999, summarized descriptions of the farm found in the Jürnjakob Swehn book [1] and added educated guesses of the most likely breeds of livestock found on the farm [12]. The article motivated me to ask two grandchildren of Carl Wiedow about the Wiedow farm [13]. Harold Wiedow and Alice (Wiedow) Wolf were children of Carl Wiedow's youngest son, Karl Heinrich, identified in the book as Hans but known later in life as Charly. Charly, married in 1910, gradually took over the farm from Carl, with Carl continuing to live on the farm until his death in 1913, and Carl's wife, Elisabeth (Wieschen), continuing to live on the farm until she moved to the home of her youngest daughter, Bertha (Berti), in Muscatine in about 1924-1925. (Figs. 7.1-7.2) Harold was born two years before and Alice six years after the death of their grandfather. Since the farm was taken over in its entirety by Charly, it seems likely that the early recollections of Harold and Alice provide us with a first-hand glimpse of Jürnjacob Swehn's "farm in Iowa."

In the chapter "Auf eigener Farm" (On my own farm), Jürnjacob Swehn writes that he owns two farms, one of 320 acres and another of 160 acres. Both Harold and Alice asserted emphatically that Grossvater had only one farm – of 160 acres. Also, the 1917 *Atlas of Iowa County, Iowa* shows only a 160-acre "Charles Wiedow Estate," occupied by Charles (Charly) Wiedow. (Fig. 7.3) The 1885 Iowa Census indicates that Carl owned the 160 acres already in 1885. Deed records show that Carl acquired 80 of these 160 acres on 7 January 1885; although I have looked, I have not yet found the deed record for the other 80 acres. Perhaps Gillhoff got the idea of an additional 320 acres from another emigrant. Harold recalls asking Grossmutter why the family bought in this hilly wooded area rather than near Victor, where the ground is level and clear of trees. She said that they were persuaded by the firewood available in Lincoln Township.

Dr. Rakow's educated guesses regarding livestock include leanings toward Yorkshire pigs and away from white Leghorn and red Rhode Island chickens, with the leanings regarding chickens influenced by the references to a black rooster in the book [2]. Harold and Alice remember Poland China, Duroc and Hampshire pigs; Buff Orphington and Plymouth Rock chickens; Shorthorn cows; also Clydesdale draft horses and a pair of smaller coach horses. The draft horses were of the breed made famous by the Budweiser Brewery Wagon. The coach horses could be used either as a team to pull a surrey or singly to pull a buggy. Harold recalls that, as a teenager, he used a horse and buggy to take Grossmutter to church and to visit the Jahlas and Roesch families. Incidentally, he did not know until I informed him that Grossmutter's mother was a Roesch. He is quite certain that Carl did not use oxen as work animals, but that Carl and Elisabeth had the usual farm cats and may have had a dog; Charly had a German Shepherd dog.

Although Carl and Elisabeth never had a good well, there were several springs on the farm. In late summer, the well and springs were often inadequate. Then Elisabeth would drive the cattle daily about one-half mile to the North English River for water.

Carl planted about an acre of fruit trees north of the house. Harold remembers excellent crops of apples, pears, peaches, plums and apricots. He remembers also gooseberries, currants and lots of grapes. The Wiedows made their own wine. Carl planted willow trees along ditches in order to grow his own fence posts.

According to family lore recalled by Susan Wehmeier, a granddaughter of Mame, Carl shared his "green thumb" with Mame's family. When visiting Mame and her family in Owosso, Michigan one summer, Carl planted numerous trees, including cherry and quince, which brought Mame's family much pleasure over many years.

Dr. Rakow notes that the Swehn letters do not mention a tractor. The lack of a tractor is not surprising. The tractor was not invented until 1892 – incidentally, by a John Froelich in Clayton County, Iowa. It seems likely that the letters from Carl Wiedow to his school teacher, Gottlieb Gillhoff, were written within a few years of 1900, at which time the use of tractors was not yet widespread. Carl never owned a tractor or a car. Charly's first tractor was a Fordson – bought about 1918-1919 – the first tractor in Iowa County. (Fig. 7.4) His first car was a 1914 Model-T Ford. (Fig. 7.5)

According to family lore, Carl Wiedow at one time ran a small "country store" from his home. For the convenience of his neighbors, he sold, among other things, basic clothing items. He gave up the store after a faulty seam in a new pair of trousers he was wearing failed one Sunday in church.

Butchering was a neighborhood event. The Wiedow barn, being the largest in the neighborhood, was typically used. Homemade wine made the event more sociable. According to a story passed down in the family, the wine flowed so freely one year that the men had troubles shooting the pigs scheduled for slaughter.

Fig. 7.1 Velda (Forney) Wiedow with their son, Clark on front porch of the Wiedow home. Clark was born in September 1915. (Photo courtesy of Sharon McKay)

Fig. 7.2 A Wiedow family gathering at the Wiedow farm in about 1929. The large window in the background is that described by Jürnjakob on page 25 of the book [2]. Front row, left to right: Adena, Alice, Violet and Mary. Back row, left to right: Clark, Velda (Forney) Wiedow, Margaret Sheppard, Elisabeth (Schröder) Wiedow, Bertha, Harold and Charly. Harold recalls the dog being a German Shepherd. (Photo courtesy of Sharon McKay)

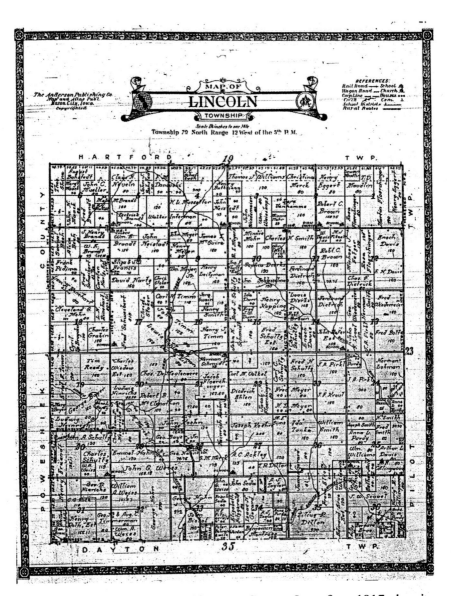

Fig. 7.3 Map of Lincoln Township, Iowa County, Iowa from 1917, showing the Charles Wiedow Estate, 160 acres, in Section 20. From Atlas of Iowa County, Iowa. Mason City, Iowa: The Anderson Publishing Co., 1917.

Fig. 7.4 This photo of a threshing machine is from a collection which contains several photos from 1919. It appears that this threshing machine did not require a tractor. (Photo courtesy of Susan Wehmeier)

Fig. 7.5 This photo is also from the collection which contains several photos from 1919. The car is probably Charly Wiedow's Model-T Ford. (Photo courtesy of Susan Wehmeier)

# Chapter 8

# THE TRAIN ACCIDENT

Verifications of events described in the Jürnjakob Swehn book but not involving the Wiedow family directly might attest to the book being based on letters from Iowa, but do not necessarily contribute to the identification of the letter writer. A dramatic example of this is the passage on p. 43 of the book [2] about the unfortunate death of Jochen Jalass. Swehn wrote: "Our Jochen story has a sad ending. After his brother got better, the two of them were going to town to trade flour for corn. A man from Alt Krenzlin in Mecklenburg was also along. They were on a cart that runs on the railroad tracks. That's something we've got here; carts that run on the tracks. But a train sneaked up on them. The other two pressed themselves thin against the wire fence along the tracks. They yelled at Jochen to press on the fence. But Jochen wanted to throw the cart off the tracks, so the train wouldn't derail. The train threw the cart off the tracks and Jochen underneath it. He only lived a few minutes. He was a mensch you could rely on. He was a really hard worker. It was too bad for him. We are all sad." In the records of the church attended by the Wiedow family one finds that Johann Joachim Jalass and Johann Albert Heinrich Seick "Würde von einem Eisenbahnzug getötet" (Were killed by a train) on 27 July 1895. It is noted that Jürnjakob mentions only the Jahlas death whereas the church records indicate two deaths. Jürnjakob might have neglected to mention the second death since this victim was not from Glaisin and hence unknown to the schoolteacher. The confirmation of Jürnjakob's account by the church records attests to the book being based on letters from Iowa.

The graduate student Kai Brauer says that he "laughed out loud" for joy when he found the entry in the church records. (Des Moines Sunday Register, 28 September 1997) His joy is understandable in the light of his desire to show that the book was a "credible historical account" rather than "pure fiction." I, on the other hand, had accepted that the book was a credible historical account from the time I first read it but was consumed by the desire to learn the identity of the letter writer. Hence I was impressed when I found the church record (already in 1988) and photographed the Jahlas gravestone (1993) but felt that the accuracy of Jürnjakob's account of the accident would contribute less to the identification of the letter writer than would personal descriptions of the writer's family.

The Johann Jalass killed in the train accident was the husband of the Mother Jahlas mentioned in the two letters addressed to the Jahlas family and reproduced in Chapter 5, and the husband of the Mrs. Jahlas and sister-in-law mentioned in the letters from Hamburg reproduced in Appendix E.

The following newspaper account of the accident was provided the author by Ferne Norris of the Poweshiek County Historical and Genealogical Society.

## Poweshiek County Republican
### (31 July 1895)

**Killed By the Cars.**--Two men named Jallas and Seik were killed on the C.&N.W., two and a half miles north of Deep River Saturday night about half-past nine o'clock. They were section hands at Guernsey and together with the section foreman they went to Deep River after some ground feed. Several sacks of this were placed on the hand-car and a little after nine o'clock they started for home. When a couple of miles north of Deep River they stopped at a crossing and listened to ascertain whether or not a train was coming. They knew that no regular train was due but they were on the look-out for extras as "wild" trains are very common on that road. After failing to hear any train the men again started toward Guernsey. They had not gone far until they were horrified at the sudden glare of a head-light coming toward them around a sharp curve. An attempt was made at once to stop the hand-car and get it off the track. The section foreman gathered a sack of feed and the others did the same thing with a view of lightening the car so they could get it off the track. The train that was approaching consisted of an engine and caboose and was running at a high rate of speed. Before the men were aware of it the train was upon them and the foreman jumped and told the men to do the same thing but they were too late. The engine struck the hand-car with terrific force and hurled it into the air. Jallas and Seik were hurled on opposite sides of the track and as soon as the train could be stopped the men were picked up and placed in the caboose. The engine ran down to Deep River after a physician but before it returned both men were dead. They were brought to Deep River where the trainmen received orders to return to Guernsey with the unfortunate men. It was about eleven o'clock before the men were taken home. In the meantime the people of Guernsey had been notified by telegraph of the sad accident and the citizens of that place were at the depot when the men were brought home. John Jallas lived in Guernsey and leaves a wife and six children to mourn his sudden taking away. Mr. Seik was married and had one child. He had not been long in this country. The news of the sad affair created much excitement both at Deep River and Guernsey and Sunday groups of men could be seen on the streets of both towns discussing the unfortunate affair.

Coroner Conaway was notified and selected a jury composed of Jacob Slaymaker, Abe L. Fry and C.F. Dunton. After taking the evidence of the engineer, fireman and conductor and also of Joseph Jallas, brother of deceased, who is the section foreman, and Drs. Grimes and Ormiston a verdict was returned that the deceased met their death from an unavoidable accident and no blame is attached to anyone.

Fig. 8.1 Gravestone of John and Dorathea Jahlas. John was the victim of the train accident; Dorathea was the Mother Jahlas mentioned in two of the letters included in Chapter 5 and the recipient of the two letters included in Appendix E. (Photo by E.L. Knuth, 1993)

# Chapter 9

# THE BOOK REVISITED

The book is recognized now to be letters from the Carl Wiedow family to the teacher of both Carl and Elisabeth, supplemented by materials from other sources. Information which I have collected regarding the Wiedow family supports that the first ten chapters in the book [2] are based either largely or entirely on letters written by the Wiedow family. In his foreword, the author acknowledges that the supplementary materials came from returnees who came through Bremen as well as from letters written by other emigrants. Brun [5] indicates that the five human-interest stories of transients told in the chapter "Working up the Corn Crop" are based on material provided by the author's oldest brother, Friedrich, who was Emigrant Missionary in Bremen from 1903 to 1915. In the best-known chapter "At my Mother's Deathbed" Johannes Gillhoff describes poignantly the death of his mother on April 8, 1905. Gillhoff shared with Krüger [10] that this chapter was for him the most effort, that the chapter went through five or six drafts before he was satisfied with it, but that it hence became the best known and did the most for the book. The chapters titled "Our School Needs a Teacher" and "Company from back Home" include undoubtedly material provided by the author's niece, Magdalene Gillhoff, who visited the USA from April 1910 to July 1912. The chapters about churches and pastors (Chapters 13-19) and the chapter "Old Stories in the New Land" appear to be collections from various sources. The grandchildren of Carl Wiedow are quite emphatic that he did not visit the 1893 World's Fair, so that the chapter "At the Chicago World's Fair" must have been based on the experiences of others. Also, the grandchildren say that they never heard of their grandfather being homesick for Mecklenburg. Hence, the chapter, "Jürnjakob, You're Homesick", is perhaps also not from Carl Wiedow.

Early editions of the book contain a final chapter "Regarding the War and the Awakening of the Germans in the States." This chapter obviously was written during the early part of WWI; it contains inflammatory remarks against the English, is critical of munitions sales by the Americans, and exaggerates the pro-German feelings of German immigrants in America.

Since Carl Wiedow died already in November 1913 and WWI did not start until July 1914, Carl Wiedow could not have written this chapter. Apparently Gillhoff became caught up in the emotions of the time and wrote it himself. It does not appear in later editions.

Krüger [10] writes that the history of the book begins in 1899 when Johannes Gillhoff received from his father a packet of letters from America. (According to a nephew of Johannes Gillhoff, these letters were destroyed after the manuscript for the book was completed in 1916.) Although this may have been the beginning of the book, much (perhaps all) of the material from the Wiedows stems from later years. In "Over the Ocean Waves," Wiedow writes that he is becoming a grandfather and that his second son now can do the farm work. Since the first three Wiedow children were married in 1899, 1901 and 1898, and since Charly was only 15 years of age in 1899, it seems likely that this letter was written after 1899. In the letter by Berti in "Indian Stories and Letters from the Children," Berti writes that she is already confirmed. Since the church records indicate that she was confirmed on April 5, 1903, her letter was written at least 4 years after 1899. Also, since Magdalena was in the USA from 1910 to 1912, her input was no earlier than 1910 and probably not until 1912.

I have found the book to be historically remarkably credible. An exception is the chapter "At my Mother's Deathbed." Early in my search for the identity of the letter writer, I seized upon the death-date information given in the chapter "At my Mother's Deathbed," hoping that it would lead me to the identity of the letter writer's mother. The book contains three pieces of information, namely that "Last Wednesday, the 12th of April, I buried my mother," an implication that his mother passed away about thirty-six years after Jürnjakob left Glaisin, and that his mother lived to seventy-two years, six months and five days. I recognized that this information is sufficient to establish both the birth and death dates within about two days. Consulting a Perpetual Calendar, I found that the 12th of April falls on Wednesday about every 6 years, e.g., in 1899, 1905 and 1911. I added the approximately thirty-six years since leaving Glaisin to the departure year 1868 and arrived at approximately 1904, which led me to select 1905 from the exemplary three years. I concluded that she must have died several days prior to April 12, 1905 and was born several days prior to October 7, 1832. My friend Myra Voss and I checked the death records in Iowa for 1905 and, to my great disappointment, found none which fit the description of Jürnjakob's mother. Years later I learned from Krüger's recollections [10] that Gillhoff had built this chapter around the death of his own mother. The Eldena church records indicate that she died on the 8th of April 1905 and was indeed buried on the 12th of April. (See

Appendix G.) According to Brun [9], she was born October 7, 1834. In this case, Gillhoff took the liberty of basing this chapter on the death of his own mother and using her burial date and age.

I have found also Trost's translation [2] of the book to be historically credible. A minor exception is found on p. 22, where Trost has assigned Schröder the first name Heine. No first name is given in the original German edition [1]. If this is indeed Elisabeth Schröder's father, then his first name was Johann. When I asked Trost about this assignment of a first name, he explained that at one time he toyed with the idea of giving several of the characters first names and then apparently overlooked Heine when, in the interest of preserving historical relevance, he went back to leaving the names as found in the original edition.

# Chapter 10

# A BROKEN HEART

Carl Wiedow's descendants are adamant in their conviction that Carl died of a broken heart. Apparently his second daughter, Lizzie, occupied a special place in her father's heart. (Having heard this, I find interesting the proximity of Lizzie to her father in Figs. 3.5 and 3.6.) She passed away unexpectedly in Aug. 1913, at the age of 33, as the result of a goiter operation which was expected to be routine, in the hospital where her brother, Henry, practiced. Her death devastated her father, known to us as Jürnjakob Swehn, who passed away then three months later at the age of 66. He died without the satisfaction of knowing how much pleasure his homespun accounts, full of wisdom, warmth, piety and humor, would bring to so many readers. Elisabeth, also known to us as Wieschen, survived him by 17 years, passing away at the age of 83 in 1930. With this introduction, the reader is encouraged to read between the lines of the following obituaries for Lizzie, Carl and Elisabeth.

---

**Obituary**
(Williamsburg Journal Tribune, Aug. 7, 1913)
Elizabeth Caroline Wiedow was born in Garnavillo, Clayton County, Iowa October 31, 1880, died at Worthington, Minn. August 1, 1913, aged 33 years, 10 months. When a year and a half old she was brought by her parents to Iowa County, near Guernsey. She was confirmed when a child in the Lutheran church and has been a faithful member ever since. She was united in marriage at the age of 18 years to Louis C. Furney, to this union was born one child, a daughter. They lived for several years on the W.E. Wilson farm near Millersburg, then went to Wisconsin, but soon came back to the old home in Guernsey where they resided at the time of her death. She leaves to mourn her loss, her husband, daughter Nola, father, mother, two sisters and two brothers. To know Lizzie was to love her. The immense throng that attended her funeral attested to the love and esteem in which she was held. She had a kind word for everyone. Funeral services were held at the Deep River church, interment in the U.B. cemetery.

69

Rev. Cole officiated at the funeral. We all unite in extending our sincere sympathy to the bereaved friends.

----

## Obituary
(Victor Record, 26 November 1913)

Carl Wiedow was born November 8, 1847, in Mecklenburg Schwerin, Germany. In 1868 he bid farewell to the old home and came to America, landing in Clayton County, Iowa. In 1871 he was united in holy wedlock with Miss Elizabeth Schroeder. In 1881 he moved to Iowa County and founded his permanent earthly home in Lincoln Township. He at once became an active member of St. John Lutheran church.

Last summer his daughter, Elizabeth, was taken from him by the cold hand of death. This filled his heart with deep sorrow.

In August he and his wife went to Muscatine to rest and gain strength. He became very ill, but after a few weeks gained enough strength to come back to his old home. After a few days his condition grew worse, and the 19th of this month he passed away peacefully at the age of 66 years and 11 days.

He leaves to mourn their loss his wife Mrs. E. Wiedow, two sons Dr. Henry Wiedow of Worthington, Minn. and Mr. Carl Wiedow on the home place and two daughters Mrs. M. Sheppard of Owosso, Mich. and Mrs. B. Nyweide of Muscatine, Iowa, and seven grandchildren, one brother and one sister.

The earthly remains were laid to rest November 21 in St. John's cemetery. Rev. Otto Kitzman, his pastor, preached the sermon from Ps. 23-4.

A very large number of relatives and friends from far and near came to pay the last respect to their departed friend.

----

## DEATH SUMMONS MRS. E. WIEDOW
### Octogenarian Was Ill For Year; To Be Buried at Victor

Mrs. Elisabeth Wiedow, 83, died at 4 o'clock this morning at the home of her daughter, Mrs. Henry Nyweide, 1021 Newell Avenue, after an illness of a year. Death was caused by complications incident to advanced age.

Born in Germany, Sept. 29, 1847, Mrs. Wiedow came to America in her early girlhood and, in 1867 was married to Charles Wiedow who died in 1913. She was a resident of Muscatine for 16 years but held a membership in the Lutheran church of Victor, Ia.

Surviving are two daughters, Mrs. Nyweide, of Muscatine and Mrs. Mary Sheppard, of Owosso, Mich., and two sons, C.H. Wiedow of Victor, Ia., and Dr. Henry Wiedow, of Pasadena, Calif. There are also 12 grandchildren surviving. One daughter, Elizabeth, preceded her mother in death.

Funeral services will be held at the home on Newell Avenue at 1 o'clock Friday afternoon with the Rev. Mr. Kreutz, of Victor, officiating. Burial will be at Victor.

Wittich Funeral home was in charge of arrangements.

# Chapter 11

# HOW DID THE KIDS DO?

In the book, three children of Jürnjakob and Wieschen are mentioned – Heinrich (the doctor), Hans and Berti. Heinrich is mentioned by name only once – in Chapter 5 [2]; usually he is referred to as the oldest son, the doctor or Berti's brother. In the chapter, "Indian Stories and Letters from the Children" [2], one finds letters from Hans and Berti.

Carl Wiedow and Elisabeth Schröder had five children – the three mentioned in the book and two more, Maria and Elisabeth. All five are now deceased, the last one in 1973. Let us take a closer look at them – and see how they fared in this "land of unlimited opportunities," keeping in mind that, had Carl Wiedow chosen to stay in Mecklenburg, his sons almost certainly would have been day laborers and his daughters wives of day laborers.

## Dr. Henry Wiedow

The life story of the oldest son, Henry, is the most interesting. We are fortunate to have available to us not only details handed down orally within the family but also written documentation in the form of a biography from 1908 [14] (Appendix B), his obituary from 1940 (Appendix C) and letters written by his adopted daughter, Edie, in 1940 and 1990 (Appendix D). For those instances in which the obituary differs from the biography, the biography is taken to be more reliable.

Henry was the only child in the family who attended high school. Since Victor did not have a high school, he attended high school in Marengo, about 12 miles from Victor. According to his biography, he enrolled at the age of 20. He must have spent several years working on the farm before he decided to continue his education. He graduated in 1897. Hence the family photograph included in Chapter 3, in which Henry's attire is quite distinguishing, might have been taken on the occasion of his high-school graduation.

He apparently entered the University in 1898. Perhaps he spent the year between graduating from high school and entering the University earning money. According to the family, he earned money for attending the University by setting traps and selling the trapped prairie chickens. At the University, he took two years of academic courses, then studied two years in the College of Medicine and received the M.D. degree April 1, 1902. Incidentally, records from the University of Iowa show that his tuition for the last two years was a total of $130. (Fig. 11.1)

He married Cora Simpson, the daughter of a neighbor to the Carl Wiedow family, July 4, 1900, i.e., during the summer between his undergraduate studies and his medical studies. (Fig. 11.2) Her salary as a school teacher helped during the early years of their marriage. Henry and Cora visited Germany three times, in 1902, in 1911 and 1913. In 1902, Henry took a special six-months course in Vienna and Berlin with Dr. Adolph Lorenz, originator of bloodless surgery, and with Dr. von Bergman, personal physician of Kaiser Wilhelm.

After returning from Europe, Henry practiced first at Round Lake, Minnesota, then opened an office in Worthington, Minnesota in 1904. (Figs. 11.3-11.4) During WWI he served as head of the Minnesota State Medical Advisory Board, for which service he was cited by President Wilson. After being diagnosed as having tuberculosis, he moved to California – first to Altadena in 1923 and then to Twentynine Palms in 1936. In the desert environment, he recovered his health quickly and embarked on the construction of a hospital for Twentynine Palms, doing much of the early construction work himself. When he passed away, the hospital had grown to where it could care for about a dozen patients. (Fig. 11.5)

Henry and Cora adopted a baby girl, Edythe Ann (Edie), in 1919. (Figs. 11.6-11.7) Her mother died at Edie's birth, in the hospital where Henry practiced. Two letters written by Edie still exist, one to her aunt Bertha (Wiedow) Nyweide shortly after Henry's death, and one to Sharon McKay, daughter of Alice (Wiedow) Wolf, in 1990. Both letters give insights to her father's career and character. For example, in her letter to Sharon, Edie writes that, by the time Henry left Worthington, his practice had expanded to include ownership of the Worthington hospital. See Appendix D.

Cora preceded Henry in death in 1928. Descendants of the Charly Wiedow family recall that a lady, known to the family as Jennie, accompanied Henry in a visit during the 1930's, and that Henry and Jennie elected to sleep in a tent pitched on the lawn. But no mention of a second marriage is found in Henry's obituaries. Recently the family discovered an inscription in Henry's gold watch, indicating that it was a present from Charles Baumer. According to family lore, Henry received the watch for graduation from high school. Hence it must have been presented in 1897. Charles Baumer died in 1907 in Marengo. In his obituary we find that, "In an unusually large sense he was a helper of men; young people, generally, received active interest from him, and he devoted no small part of his Christian work to the finding of the Way for young people whom he could bring under his affectionate influence." Hopefully he became aware before he died that Henry had graduated from the University and had established a successful practice.

In the obituary for Dr. Wiedow we read that he was found dead under his overturned coupe. He had left the hospital a few minutes earlier, remarking to his daughter that he was tired but still had three calls to make. He had a lifelong fascination for cars, and held driver's license No. 1 in Nobles County, Minnesota. (Fig. 11.8) It is symbolic that he died in his beloved car on the way to helping beloved suffering patients. The high esteem with which he was held in the community is voiced in the editorial (Appendix C) which appeared in the local newspaper after his death.

## Maria (Mame) Wiedow

I found the life story of the oldest daughter, Maria (Mame), also unusually interesting, especially in view of her strong (dominating?) influence on her children and grandchildren. (Fig. 11.9) Although she didn't attend high school, she had the highest regard for advanced education. She married a bone specialist, Dr. Cary Sheppard. And she was adamant that their three daughters would attend not only high school but also the University. Dr. Sheppard established his practice in Owosso, Michigan. When the time came for the daughters to attend the University, Mame established for herself and the three daughters a second residence in Ann Arbor, home of the University of Michigan. All three girls earned not only the B.A. Degree but also the M.A. Degree.

All three girls married university graduates. These three families provided Mame with four grandchildren, and all but one of these grandchildren earned at least one university degree.

The family of Mame's oldest daughter, Margaret, is for me the most interesting. She married Hobart Willard, who received a Ph.D. in analytical chemistry from Harvard University in 1909. He was for many years Professor of Chemistry at the University of Michigan, and is widely known for his determination of the atomic weight of Lithium and for his researches on the benefits of fluorine in drinking water. They have two daughters; both became teachers. The youngest, Nancy, is also a writer – she has published more than 20 books. In the book, Cracked Corn and Snow Ice Cream, she collected stories and photos of her ancestors. Quotes from this book are included in Chapter 15. Among the photos in the book, one finds a photo of Carl Wiedow's barn.

Without question, the Sheppard-Wiedow family became an unusually learned family. And this happened simply as a result of Mame's convictions regarding the value of advanced education – in the "land of unlimited opportunities."

## Elisabeth (Lizzie) Wiedow

The second daughter, Elisabeth, was mentioned already in connection with the death of Carl Wiedow. (Fig. 11.10) She died prematurely and unexpected in August 1913 at the age of 33 in Henry's hospital, on the occasion of a goiter operation which should not have been dangerous. She was married to Louis Furney, a carpenter. (Fig. 11.11) Since she was the first child to marry (1898), she could have been the source of Jürnjakob's comment that he is beginning to become a grandfather. Lizzie and Louis had two children; the first died early, and the family apparently has lost contact with the second one. A sad ending to a sad story.

## Karl (earlier Hans, later Charly) Wiedow

The second son was baptized Karl Heinrich Wilhelm. In the book, we find a letter from Hans. Perhaps he used Hans since at that time the names Karl (Charly) and Heinrich (Henry) were pre-empted at home by his father and his brother. Later in life he went by Charly. His interests included photography and hunting. (Fig. 11.12) He married Velda Forney, a niece to his sister Elisabeth's husband – they had seven children. (Figs. 7.1 and 11.13) He stayed on the home place until the Great Depression; in 1936 he was unable to meet payments which were due, moved to Deep River and became a cabinet maker. One of their children, Harold, still lives near the home place.

My first face-to-face meeting with the Wiedow family, May 1993, was with Harold, Alice (nee Wiedow) Wolf and Alice's daughter, Sharon. Especially Harold, born in 1911, related much about Grossvater and Grossmutter Wiedow, i.e., about Carl and Elisabeth), including that Grossvater had helped with the building of the church. He mentioned explicitly the building of the steeple. We now know why. Recently someone found a photo taken during the construction of the steeple (Fig. 11.14). It is apparently from 1895. If one looks very closely, one sees two workers high up on the scaffolding. Harold understands that one of them is Grossvater Wiedow.

In the book we find also a letter from Hans to the schoolteacher in Glaisin. Hans wrote about the schools – about a German school, i.e., St. John's school, and about an English school, i.e., a public school. The old church school building has been replaced by a new building. The small public school building, Lincoln Township No. 4, is located a short distance north of the old home place (Fig. 3.8 and 11.15); it has not been in use for many years and has recently collapsed. Many local people are not aware of its existence.

## Bertha (Berti) Wiedow

In the book we find also a letter to the schoolteacher from Swehn's daughter Berti. Berti is certainly Carl Wiedow's youngest daughter Bertha. She moved to Muscatine, Iowa after her marriage with Henry Nyweide, a bakery driver from Muscatine, and lived there until her death in 1973. (Fig. 11.16) One notes with interest that Berti mentions a visit to Muscatine in her letter.

In 1996, en route to Iowa from a reunion of my WWII outfit in Peoria, Illinois, I stopped in Muscatine and visited Bill Nyweide, a grandson of Bertha; he still lives in the house where Bertha and family had lived. They still have an old steamer trunk with "Wiedow" carved into the top. (Fig. 11.17) Bill graciously provided me with a copy of a letter written in 1940 by Edie Wiedow (adopted daughter of Henry) to her Aunt Bertha. See Appendix D. Bertha and Henry Nyweide had a son, Charly – named after his grandfather. In her later years, Elisabeth Wiedow (AKA Wieschen) made her home with Bertha. She died there in 1930.

## Summary

In the book, Jürnjakob Swehn wrote, "In the village, regardless of how hard I worked, I would have been always a day laborer, at best a cottager, and my children would have become day laborers. - - - Here I have made myself free. Here I stand with my feet on my own land and don't work for the farmers." This passage certainly fits Carl Wiedow and his children. Carl Wiedow didn't remain a day laborer – and the children certainly did not become day laborers!

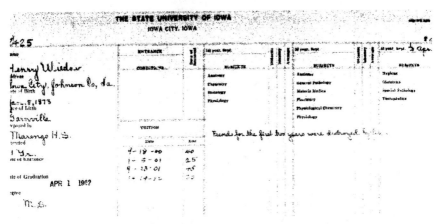

Fig. 11.1  Transcript from the College of Medicine, University of Iowa, Iowa City, Iowa.  Date of graduation -- April 1, 1902.

Fig. 11.2  Henry and Cora (Simpson) Wiedow.  (Photo courtesy of Sharon McKay)

Fig. 11.3  Henry and Cora in Minnesota, 1902.  (Photo courtesy of William Welch)

Fig. 11.4 Henry's horses and buggy, Minnesota, 1902. (Photo courtesy of William Welch)

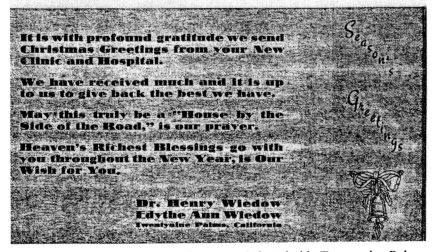

It is with profound gratitude we send Christmas Greetings from your New Clinic and Hospital.

We have received much and it is up to us to give back the best we have.

May this truly be a "House by the Side of the Road," is our prayer.

Heaven's Richest Blessings go with you throughout the New Year, is Our Wish for You.

Dr. Henry Wiedow
Edythe Ann Wiedow
Twentynine Palms, California

Season's Greetings

Fig. 11.5 Christmas card depicting Henry's hospital in Twentynine Palms, California. (Photo courtesy of Susan Wehmeier)

*Eldon L. Knuth*

Fig. 11.6 Henry and daughter Edie, Altadena, California, 1926. (Photo courtesy of William Welch)

Fig. 11.7 Henry, daughter Edie and their dogs Blondie, Topsy and Wags, Twentynine Palms, California, 1940, shortly before Henry's death. (Photo courtesy of William Welch)

Fig. 11.8  Cora and Henry in his 1918 Buick, his nurse to the left.  (Photo courtesy of Sharon McKay)

Fig. 11.9 A Wiedow family gathering in about 1917. Front row, from left to right: Mary Wiedow, Harriet Sheppard, Elisabeth (Schröder) Wiedow, Mame (Wiedow) Sheppard, Bernice Sheppard, Harold Wiedow. Back row, from left to right: Henry Wiedow, Margaret Sheppard, Bertha (Wiedow) Nyweide.

Fig. 11.10 Elisabeth (Wiedow) Furney (Photo courtesy of Sharon McKay)

Fig. 11.11 After the hunt. Louis Furney, husband of Elisabeth Wiedow, on left. (Photo courtesy of Sharon McKay)

Fig. 11.12 Charly Wiedow with his hunting rifle. (Photo courtesy of Sharon McKay)

Fig. 11.13 Lamb and three daughters of Charly and Velda (Forney) Wiedow in the back yard of the Wiedow farm. Left to right: Alice, Violet and Adena Wiedow. (Photo courtesy of Sharon McKay)

Fig. 11.14 St. John's Lutheran Church under construction in 1895. One of the men visible on the scaffolding is Carl Wiedow. (Photo courtesy of Sharon McKay)

Fig. 11.15 Alice (Wiedow) Wolf in Schoolhouse No. 4, where she went to school as a child. Arithmetic problems, from the distant past, are still visible on the blackboard she is holding. (Photo courtesy of Sharon McKay)

Fig. 11.16 Bertha (Wiedow) Nyweide at her home in Muscatine, Iowa. Her grandson, Bill Nyweide, says she was particularly fond of this blossoming tree. (Photo courtesy of Bill Nyweide)

Fig. 11.17 Steamer trunk with "Wiedow" carved into its top. In possession of Bill Nyweide. (Photo by E.L. Knuth, 1996)

# Chapter 12

# PARENTS, BROTHERS AND SISTERS

Parents of Carl Wiedow

    The rest of Carl Wiedow's family – his parents (Joachim and Sophie), his younger brother, and his sister – emigrated in 1870, two years after Carl. They received written consent to emigrate on March 26, 1870, boarded the ship Friedeburg in Hamburg, arrived in New York on May 31, and settled in Garnavillo Township, Clayton County, Iowa in time to be counted in the U.S. Census on July 12. After the 1870 Census, no trace is found of Joachim until June 1884, when he appears in the list of communicants at St. John's Church in Victor, Iowa County, Iowa. Then he appears regularly in the communicant list until his death on January 19, 1888. Although his death is recorded in the St. John's Church records, no gravestone is found for him in the St. John's Cemetery.

    Sophie is listed as a baptism sponsor for Carl Wiedow's second child, baptized September 6, 1874 in Garnavillo. In spite of numerous efforts by several researchers, in Clayton County, in Iowa County, in Poweshiek County and in Mecklenburg, no trace of Sophie after 1874 has been found. The failure to find both Joachim and Sophie in the 1880 U.S. Census is particularly puzzling.

Brother of Carl Wiedow

    Carl Wiedow's younger brother, Johann Carl Friedrich, emigrated to America with his parents and sister in 1870. But, contrary to Carl's emigration, Johann did it with permission. He obtained a written release from compulsory military service on March 16, 1870 for the purpose of emigrating to America; he was then 19 years of age. Permission to emigrate was included in that for his parents. In the 1870 U.S. Census, he is found with his parents in Garnavillo Township, Clayton County, Iowa.

    Johann married Wilhelmine Müller in Garnavillo on March 29, 1875. In the church records, his family name is written Widoo. A daughter,

Wilhelmine Caroline Margarethe, was born to them November 4, 1876. In the 1880 U.S. Census, John Vedo, wife Minnie and daughter Minnie are found in Grand Meadow Township, Clayton County, Iowa, either in or near the village of Springfield. (Springfield was founded in 1869, but died out already many years ago. Fig. 2.2 )

After locating John and Minnie in the 1880 U.S. Census, I was stymied, for about a decade, in my efforts to follow them further. In the meanwhile, a granddaughter of the daughter Minnie had approached me in her search for family details. Those details which she did have were intriguing. Her grandmother had been raised by the grandmother's uncle and aunt, Louis and Caroline (Mueller) Meyer, Caroline being a sister of her mother, Minnie (Mueller) Wiedow. Furthermore, both her mother and grandmother had refused to talk about the grandmother's background, and became visibly upset if anyone inquired about it.

I had found a marriage record in Clayton Center, Clayton County for a Johann Wiedow and Maria Schrodt dated February 21, 1881. A daughter, Marie Hennriette, born thirteen days earlier was baptized on the same day as the marriage. I had filed it with my records for the Johann Wiedow - Sophia Heidtmann family (Appendix F), allowing that the groom might be their son, Johan, born May 13, 1859. Furthermore, it seemed unlikely that the groom would be the John Vedo who was listed as married in the U.S. Census dated June 1, 1880. Then, in October 1998, I visited Clayton County once again – on the occasion of my high school class reunion celebrating the 55th anniversary of our graduation – and stumbled upon the key to the puzzle. While browsing through the records for the St. Paul Lutheran Church in Postville, Iowa (located adjacent to Grand Meadow Township), I found (translated here into English):

"October 10, 1880. Buried: Wilhelmina Wido, born January 15, 1855 in Stolp, Prussian Pommern. Died October 8, 1880 at the age of 25 years, 8 months and 23 days. She leaves behind a husband and a child. Died from consumption (tuberculosis)."

This exciting clue prompted a re-examination of the Wiedow-Schrodt marriage. In the 1900 U.S. Census, I found John and Mary Wedow living in Deep River Township, Poweshiek County, Iowa – not far from the Carl Wiedow farm. Records from the nearby St. John's Church confirmed that the Mary in this census was Mary Schrodt. The census records indicated that John was born in January 1851, the birth month and year of Carl Wiedow's brother. Furthermore, Harold Wiedow, grandson of Carl Wiedow recalls that this John Wiedow was the brother of his grandfather. We see that Johann Wiedow did indeed remarry four months after the death of his first wife. And we see now also why Minnie, the child of Johann Wiedow's first marriage, was raised by her uncle and aunt – and why she refused to talk about her background. The loss of her mother and the separation from her father at the age of 4 must have been traumatic.

Apparently John and Mary moved to Poweshiek County soon after their marriage; their second child was baptized at St. John's in 1883. They had a total of four children; a descendant of their oldest child has contacted me, inquiring about family details. Mary died Oct. 29, 1903 at the age of 48. The church record of her death is unusually detailed and candid, indicating that she died from a heart attack brought on by the stress of chasing cattle out of a cornfield; also that she was not well-informed and was weak in faith. John died March 3, 1930 at the age of 79. According to the records of St. John's, Mary is buried in Lot 28 of St. John's Cemetery; the Poweshiek County death records indicate that John is buried in the Guernsey Cemetery. Neither grave has a marker.

According to stories passed down by descendants of Carl Wiedow, the Carl Wiedow family sometimes disapproved of John Wiedow's treatment of his family. For example, they were critical of John for having his wife caulk by hand the spaces between the stones in the walls of their basement.

Another human interest side of John Wiedow: At the time that the two descendants of John Wiedow contacted me, the descendant from the first marriage had never heard about the second marriage; the descendant from the second marriage had never heard about the first marriage. With prior agreement from both, I was pleased to bring them in contact with each other.

## Sister of Carl Wiedow

The search for Carl Wiedow's sister, Anna Maria Elisabeth, has many parallels to that for his brother. Born in 1853, she also emigrated two years after Carl, was included in the permission to emigrate obtained by her parents, traveled with them to New York, and is listed with her parents and brother in the 1870 U.S. Census. I had found marriage records for Heinrich Schrank and Marie Wido (Clayton Center, March 14, 1873) and for Heinrich Schuldt and Marie Schrank (Clayton Center, July 16, 1875) already early in my searches. I had filed also these records with my records for the Johann Wiedow - Sophia Heidtmann family (Appendix F), allowing that the bride might be Sophia Heidtmann's illegitimate daughter, Maria Dorethea Friederike, born in Germany in 1843 and confirmed in Garnavillo in 1858. Not only was the Heidtmann daughter named Maria, but also I expected marriage at age 29 to be more likely than marriage at age 19. Again I was stymied for about a decade. Then, motivated by the mention of a surviving sister in Carl Wiedow's obituary (1913), I re-examined the Schuldt-Wiedow family. In the 1900 U.S. Census, I found Henry and Mary Shulz living in Saratoga Township, Howard County, Iowa. The census records indicated that Mary was born in August 1853, the birth month and year of Carl Wiedow's sister; the six children listed in the census corresponded to six of the nine Schuldt-Wiedow children baptized at Clayton Center. Success!

The 1900 U.S. Census indicates that Heinrich Schuldt was born in December 1837. The passenger list for the Steamship Hammonia for departure from Hamburg on 13 May 1868 includes a Heinrich Schuldt, age 30, born in Gross Schmölen. The Dömitz church records document that a Johann Jürgen Heinrich Schult was born in Gross Schmölen on 10 December 1837, in agreement with the month and year given in the 1900 Census.

According to the 1910 U.S. Census, Mary and three of her children (Henry, Herman and Will) were living in Chester Township, Howard County, Iowa. The records indicate also that Mary was married, that is, she was not a widow. But where was her husband?

In summary: Maria (AKA Marie and Mary) married Heinrich Schrank in 1873; they lived in Farmersburg Township, Clayton County, where a daughter was born in 1874; Heinrich died in May 1875. In July, two months later, Maria married Heinrich Schuldt; they lived until at least 1897 in Giard Township, Clayton County, where nine children were born in the time period from 1876 until 1896; they moved to Howard County before 1900 and Mary lived there until at least 1910.

In the Cemetery Listings for Clayton County, Iowa compiled by the WPA (Works Projects Administration) in 1935-1942 we find a "Mother" Schuldt, 1850-1914, buried in the Giard Cemetery, Giard. Since Maria (Wiedow) Schuldt was born in 1853, lived in Giard from about 1875 until at least 1897, and was still alive in 1913 (according to the obituary of her brother Carl Wiedow), it seems likely that she and this "Mother Schuldt" are one and the same. Attempts to obtain additional details from the Giard Cemetery have been stymied by a report that the Giard Cemetery records were burned by the widow of the record keeper after he passed away!

The descendants of Carl and Johann Wiedow with whom I am in contact were surprised to learn that Carl and Johann had a sister; apparently the several families had not stayed in contact. I have not yet made contact with descendants of the Schuldt-Wiedow family.

## Parents of Elisabeth Schröder

Elisabeth (Wieschen in the book) and her parents, Johann and Maria (also known by her third given name, Dorothea), came to America together. They conformed to the required formalities and received written consent to emigrate on August 5, 1868. They crossed the Atlantic aboard the steamer Germania, arriving in New York on October 15, 1868. The first trace found of the parents in Iowa is in the 1870 U.S. Census, which documents that they were farming in Volga Township, Clayton County. Also with them were their son, John, and a hired man, Charles Remer. Remer was also from Glaisin; I am in contact with a grandson and a granddaughter of Remer. According to the 1880 U.S. Census, the parents and their son John were still in Volga Township at that time.

Johann died in Farmersburg, Clayton County, March 14, 1882 of a stroke and is buried in the old Garnavillo Cemetery. The gravestone, although now in two pieces, still exists.

Maria died at the Carl Wiedow home in Iowa County March 30, 1903 at age 81. She was survived by 4 children, 22 grandchildren and 10 great grandchildren. She is buried in the St. John's Cemetery at Victor, not with her husband at Garnavillo.

## Siblings of Elisabeth Schröder

Elisabeth's parents had 8 children. Four of them, including a pair of twins, died in infancy, a reflection of the state of medical care at that time. The remaining four, including Elisabeth, reached Iowa.

The two oldest girls, Maria and Wilhelmine, arrived in New York from Hamburg aboard the ship Saxonia on May 21, 1868 – five months in advance of their parents and Elisabeth. Maria married Karl Ahrends, from Ludwigslust, Mecklenburg, on October 22, 1868 in Garnavillo, one week after her parents and Elisabeth arrived in New York. The family is found in Volga Township in the 1880 U.S. Census, in Read Township in the 1900 U.S. Census and in Garnavillo Township in the 1910 U.S. Census. Karl was a farmer; they had 6 children.

Wilhelmine married John Schult on August 20, 1868 – two months before her parents and Elisabeth arrived in America. John was born in Göhlen, Mecklenburg, but his family lived later in Glaisin. John and Wilhelmine certainly knew each other already in Glaisin. The family farmed in Garnavillo Township according to the 1870 U.S. Census and in Hartford Township, Iowa County according to the 1880 and 1900 U.S. Census. They had 9 children.

According to the 1900 U.S. Census, Elisabeth's brother John emigrated already in 1867. Indeed, in the passenger lists, we find that a Joh. Schröder, age 18, arrived in New York on 5 Oct. 1867 aboard the SS Weser. He was the first of the Schröder family to arrive in America, arriving even ahead of Carl Wiedow. His obituary indicates that he and his parents settled first in Michigan. However, at the time of the 1870 U.S. Census, he was living with his parents in Volga Township, Clayton County, Iowa. He married Maria Bartels on January 9, 1878 in Elkport, Clayton County, Iowa. She immigrated in 1870 and is not the Maria Bartels from Glaisin who immigrated in 1882. The 1880 U.S. Census indicates that John, Maria and Maria's mother were living on the farm with John's parents. Sometime later, John and family followed his sisters Wilhelmine (married to Schult) and Elisabeth (married to Wiedow) to Iowa County, where he farmed in Hartford Township until his retirement to Marengo, also in Iowa County. Two photos of family gatherings which include John and Maria are included here as Figs. 12.1 and 12.2. Fig. 12.2 is unusually interesting since it includes Elisabeth (see also Fig. 12.3), her brother, and three of her four living children. John died September 17, 1927 in Marengo and is buried there. John and Maria had 6 children.

In summary, we see that all four of the Schröder children established homes in America. The son became a farmer and all three daughters were married to farmers. Altogether, the four families had 26 children, of which 22 were still alive when their Grossmutter Schröder passed away in 1903. Adding to these grandchildren the 15 children of Carl Wiedow's siblings, we wonder how many relatives of Carl and Elisabeth are living today in Iowa!

From a broader view, we see that the Wiedow and Schröder families, including the seven children, settled first in Clayton County. All of the children excepting the Ahrends-Schröder family eventually moved farther west, most of them in or near Iowa County. Clayton County, particularly the area around Garnavillo and Clayton Center, was the goal of many of the earlier Iowa settlers because it had good farmland and was close to the Mississippi River. When farmland became scarce and more expensive in Clayton County, many farmers moved either northward (toward Postville) or westward.

Fig. 12.1 A Wiedow-Schröder family outing in Muscatine, Iowa in 1919. From left to right: Unidentified, Bernice Sheppard, Mame (Wiedow) Sheppard, Elisabeth (Schröder) Wiedow, Bertha (Wiedow) Nyweide, Mary (Bartels) Schröder and John Schröder. Front: Charles Nyweide (Photo courtesy of Susan Wehmeier)

Fig. 12.2 A Wiedow-Schröder family gathering in about 1925, apparently on the Wiedow farm. Front row, from left to right: Bernice Sheppard, Margaret Sheppard, Adena Wiedow, Mame (Wiedow) Sheppard (front and center!), Alice Wiedow, Velda (Forney) Wiedow. Middle row, from left to right: Mary Wiedow, Violet Wiedow, Elisabeth (Schröder) Wiedow, Mary (Bartels) Schröder, Cora (Simpson) Wiedow, and Bertha (Wiedow) Nyweide. Back row, from left to right: Charles Nyweide, Henry Nyweide, Henry Wiedow (with dapper bow tie) and John Schröder. (Photo courtesy of Susan Wehmeier)

Fig. 12.3 Elisabeth (Schröder) Wiedow, AKA Wieschen, in about 1925, at about 77 years of age. This photo was taken perhaps at the family gathering depicted in the previous photo. (Photo courtesy of Susan Wehmeier)

# Chapter 13

# ROOTS AND BRANCHES

After I had shown that Swehn was indeed a Wiedow, I became curious about Carl Wiedow's ancestors. Since both of our families had roots in Mecklenburg, were we perhaps related? Furthermore, if I didn't do the genealogy for the Wiedow family, someone else would! So I set for myself the goal of publishing the Wiedow-family genealogy at the same time that I revealed the identity of the letter writer. Working largely with the records available through the Family History Center in Los Angeles, I assembled an Ahnentafel (family tree) and family sheets. (A family sheet is a summary of genealogy data for one family presented in tabular form. When my wife first heard the expression "family sheet," she wondered if it had anything to do with bed linens!) The Ahnentafel, in the form of a family tree for Carl Wiedow's oldest son, is given in Appendix A. The data are from churchbooks in Berge, Conow, Eldena, Gorlosen, Grabow, Groß Laasch, Groß Pankow and Muchow, and from the Mecklenburg Census from 1819. Even though fifteen years have passed since I began my studies of the the Wiedow-family genealogy, this Ahnentafel is nevertheless still presented as a status report.

The preparation of the Ahnentafel was complicated by the spelling, in the earlier records, of the family name according to the pronunciation. The pastor in Grabow wrote sometimes *Wiede*, sometimes *Wiedow*; the pastor in Conow wrote *Wiede*; and the pastor in Eldena wrote *Wiedow*. In the Mecklenburg Census from 1819, one finds even *Wiese*. For help with the sorting and correlating of the data for the various name forms, I am grateful to Rolf Gödecke (Hamburg), the late Dr. Günther Schröder (Göttingen) and Friedrich-Wilhelm Witt (Radolfzell am Bodensee), all of whom also have close ties to Mecklenburg. The late Dr. Günther Schröder had a two-fold personal interest in the Jürnjakob Swehn book. The most obvious interest was a possible relationship to Wieschen Schröder. The second interest was a possible relationship between his grandmother, a Busacker, and the Busacker family mentioned in the book. Although we found that the Knuth family is related to Wieschen, common ancestors being the Sass-Meier couple in the 7th (!) generation of the Wiedow

Ahnentafel, we never did find a relationship between Dr. Schröder and the Wiedow-Schröder family.

I was able to trace the paternal branch of Carl Wiedow's Ahnentafel back only three generations, i.e., back only to his greatgrandfather, Ernst Joachim Christian Wiede, so identified in the baptism records of his children in Kleeste, Brandenburg. His occupation is given as Hütmann, i.e., herdsman. The limited number of openings for herdsmen in a given village required frequently that the son of a herdsman take a job in another village. This makes tracing their ancestories a more challenging task than for firmly rooted families. In Chapter 4 I mentioned that Johann Rösch was an uncle of Elisabeth (Schröder) Wiedow. A four-generation descendancy chart for Hans Jochim Rösch is included in Appendix A in order to help visualize this relationship.

Family property and family status passed usually to the oldest son. As an example, let's examine Elisabeth Schröder's forefathers. Her greatgreatgrandfather, Adolph, was a Schulze (mayor). Her greatgrandfather, Christian, was apparently the oldest son and became also a Schulze. Her grandfather, Daniel Hinrich, was the second son and had to be content with becoming a Hauswirth (landlord). Her father, Johann Jochim Heinrich, was the fourth son and became a Häusler (worker in a cottage industry). The records in Mecklenburg confirm that the economic opportunities in America were certainly important for the emigration of both the Wiedow and the Schröder families. For those cases in which the records indicate the profession, the profession is given also in the Ahnentafel. We see that Carl Wiedow's father, Joachim, was a Tagelöhner (day laborer) and that Elisabeth Schröder's father, Johann, was a Häusler. Neither could hope to improve his status. Similarly, many workers in Mecklenburg lacked assurance of a reasonable standard of living. This hopeless condition drove many to emigrate to America, to the "land of unlimited opportunities."

# Chapter 14

# JÜRNJAKOB SWEHN PROJECTS

### The Jürnjakob Swehn Photo Project

In 1997, three professional photographers from Mecklenburg-Vorpommern (MV), namely Harry Hardenberg from Stralsund, Walter Hinghaus from Schwerin and Bernd Lasdin from Neubrandenburg, all graduates of the Leipzig School for Graphics and Book Art, organized a Jürnjakob Swehn Photo Project. The aim of the project was to renew ties between the people of MV and the USA by exhibiting photos from MV in the USA and then exhibiting photos from the USA in MV. Hinghaus had learned of my interest in Jürnjakob Swehn from an editor at Stock and Stein, publishers of the magazine Mecklenburg, fortuitously also located in Schwerin. I had submitted my first manuscript [17] to Mecklenburg in June of 1997. The photographers had already written a proposal to the state of MV for financial assistance during a four-week visit to the USA, and wondered if I would be willing to assist them, e.g., with arrangements and translation. Since all three had grown up in East Germany, they had done little traveling outside East Germany and had learned very little English. For me, the timing was excellent – the combination of introducing the photographers and presenting results of my researches was a natural. So I agreed with pleasure to assist them during their stay in Iowa. They subsequently received a modest 15,000-Mark grant from MV, and the Project became a reality. They brought 90 photo enlargements to the USA and spent one week each in Iowa, Milwaukee, Charlotte (Mecklenburg County, North Carolina) and New York, exhibiting and photographing. Arrangements in Iowa were facilitated by the enthusiastic genealogist, Myra Voss, a long-time friend and President of the Clayton County Chapter of the Iowa Genealogical Society. Highlights were the presentations in the church in Clayton Center (Clayton County), where the third child of Carl Wiedow and Elisabeth Schröder was baptized (Fig. 14.1), and in the church in Victor (Iowa County), where the Wiedows went to church after about 1881 (Fig. 14.2). These presentations included an introduction to the book [1], a reading of selections from those portions of the book which I had translated, an account of my search for Jürnjakob's identity, an exhibit of the photos from MV and the taking of photos. The presentation in Clayton Center was held on the same weekend as the annual Germanfest in nearby Monona; the photographers experienced and photographed also this Iowa version of the Munich Oktoberfest. Photos selected from the more than 10,000 taken in the USA have been exhibited in Glaisin, Schwerin, Stralsund and Berlin.

## Translation of the Book

It was during this 1997 visit to Iowa that I first met Dick and Betty Trost. Already at the Clayton Center presentation, Larry Allan, editor of the Hawkeye Heritage, mentioned to me that Pastor Trost had begun a translation of the book. Two days later, at the Victor presentation, Dick and Betty introduced themselves. We explored our mutual interest in the book – addressing specifically that we had both started translating the book. Dick mentioned incidentally that Prof. Kamphoefner had started translating the book in about 1991 but had dropped the project when he learned that Dick was already doing it. Dick was invited to participate in the program. My presentation included several paragraphs from what I had translated; after my presentation, Dick read several paragraphs from what he had translated. Our translations were an obvious duplication of effort! Before parting that day, we agreed that he would continue with his translation and that I would focus my attention on the identification and characterization of the letter writer. His translation [2] appeared in print three years later. I would like to think that my interest in the book accelerated his translation; apparently, whereas the first one-third of the translation took more than six years, the last two-thirds took less than three years! Now, eight years later, I am combining and expanding into the present publication the several progress reports on my researches which I have either presented or published since October 1997.

## The Johannes Gillhoff Society

The Johannes Gillhoff Society, founded in 1993 [15], seeks to propagate the literary legacy of Johannes Gillhoff, to document the emigration from Glaisin and surroundings to America, and to preserve the local customs and history. The members converted a classroom of the old schoolhouse into a small museum which is called die Gillhoff-Stuv (The Gillhoff Room). See Fig. 14.3. Hartmut Brun contributed details and displays regarding the life and legacy of Johannes Gillhoff – Udo Baarck provided data and exhibits which document the emigration from Glaisin to America. Both are founding members of the Society. In cooperation with the Kulturkreis Mecklenburg e.V. (Mecklenburg Culture Bureau) , the Society hosts annually the Gillhoff-Days during the second weekend in June. In 1998 the theme of the Gillhoff-Days was "Striving for One's Own Land and House," i.e., the same as the central theme of the book [1]. Hartmut Brun addressed "Johannes Gillhoff as Author of the Novel 'Jürnjakob Swehn, der Amerikafahrer'," Udo Baarck and Kai Brauer spoke on Paths to 'Jürnjakob Swehn'," and I answered the question "Who was 'Jürnjakob Swehn'." At the invitation of the Society, the material presented here in Chapters 11-13 was presented at subsequent Gillhoff Days in 1999-2001. In order to further the documentation of the emigration from Glaisin and surroundings to America, Baarck visited Minnesota and Iowa in October 1998, taking with him an Emigration List from Glaisin. I had the pleasure of hosting his visit to Clayton County, Iowa. The timing was such that Baarck was able to experience also my high-school class-reunion dinner and the annual local Germanfest. He found so many documents and immigrant descendants relevant to the Immigration List that he returned in 1999 and 2001 to continue his searches.

## A Jürnjakob Swehn Class Project

At the end of the 1997-98 school year, a group of students at the Goethe Gymnasium in Schwerin visited an exhibit by Walter Hinghaus of photos taken during the abovementioned Jürnjakob Swehn Photo Project. The photos generated a desire to "see for themselves." The following fall, under the guidance of instructor Cornelia Heine, 15 students organized a project which they named "Die Amerika-Fahrer (The Travellers to America)." The project name was a deliberate take-off on the name of the book, "Jürnjakob Swehn, der Amerikafahrer." They divided into three groups which were assigned the tasks of (a) collecting names, addresses and destinations of emigrants from records in Schwerin, Hamburg and Bremen, (b) seeking out, largely via the internet, others with interests in emigration and/or in Swehn and (c) seeking out support for a class trip to the USA, including to the neighborhood where the Carl Wiedow family lived. My contact with the class began in February 1999. The most challenging task for the class was raising funds for the trip to the USA. They took advantage of the 250th anniversary of the birth of Goethe and the 50th anniversary of the founding of their school to organize and staff a Goethe Cafe for the six-day celebration of the school founding. The Cafe was seen as such a success (also financially) that it motivated contributions to their travel funds in the form of donations. Additional funds were raised by participating in a traffic count for the state of Mecklenburg. The Project culminated in a ten-day trip to America in September 1999. They visited Des Moines (hosted by Pastor Trost), St. John's church in Victor (where Carl Wiedow attended church and was buried), Milwaukee (one of the largest German settlements in America), Clayton County (hosted by Myra Voss) and Chicago (a big American city). See Fig. 14.4. I had the pleasure of helping with the arrangements for the visit to Clayton County, where the class slept at the Voss farmhouse and attended a high-school homecoming football game and dance at Elkader. They wrote back that the trip "war einfach toll! (was simply fantastic!)"

## Eldena 775-Year Anniversary

In July 2004, the village of Eldena celebrated the 775-year anniversary of the founding of a nunnery at the village site in 1229. The celebration included an historical evening on Friday the 2nd of July, a parade on Saturday the 3rd of July and the publishing of a 233-page <u>Chronik Eldena, 1229-2004</u> (Chronicle of Eldena, 1229-2004). The historical evening included talks by the village historian Marina Kappe (introduction to Eldena history, emigration), Udo Baarck from Glaisin (emigration from Eldena), Friedrich-Wilhelm Witt from Radolfzell (early recollections of Eldena), Eldon Knuth from California (emigration from Mecklenburg, Jürnjakob Swehn) and Rolf Goedecke from Hamburg (computers as a tool for genealogy). The highlight of my presentation was the reading of a greeting from Harold Wiedow, a grandson of Carl Wiedow and Elisabeth Schröder (AKA Jürnjakob Swehn and Wieschen Schröder), to the members of the congregation. See Fig. 14.5. The parade theme was the history of Eldena. Of special interest to the author was a float depicting the sailing of Carl Wiedow to America. See Fig. 14.6. The writing on the sails of the ship translates into: "Carl Wiedow seeks his fortune in America. 1847 - born in Bellevue, baptized in Eldena. 1868 - emigrated from Glaisin to America. Carl Wiedow is Jürnjakob Swehn." Carl Wiedow is indeed now a part of the history of Eldena!

Fig. 14.1 Zion Lutheran Church, Clayton Center, Iowa. Dedicated in 1874. Elisabeth, third child of Carl and Elisabeth Wiedow, was baptized here in 1879. (Photo by E.L. Knuth, 1997)

Fig. 14.2  Descendants of Carl and Elisabeth Wiedow in attendance at the Oct. 6, 1997 pesentation at St. John's Lutheran Church, Victor, Iowa. Standing, from left to right: Violet (Wiedow) Wise, Sharon (Wolf) McKay, Alice (Wiedow) Wolf, Donald McKay, Harold Wiedow, Clark Wiedow. Seated, from left to right: Kyle McKay, Alicia McKay.  (Photo by E.L. Knuth, 1997)

Fig. 14.3 Johannes Gillhoff commemorative stone at the old schoolhouse in Glaisin, Mecklenburg. Photo made on occasion of visit by author (also in photo) in 1997. (Photo by M. Knuth)

*Eldon L. Knuth*

Fig. 14.4 "Die Amerika-Fahrer" (The Travellers to America), from the Goethe Gymnasium, Schwerin, Mecklenburg, at St. John's Lutheran Church, Victor, Iowa, Sept. 21, 1999. (Photo courtesy of Cornelia Heine)

112

The Year 2004

Dear Members of the Eldena Congregation!

As a grandson of two earlier members of the Eldena congregation, namely Carl Wiedow and his wife Elisabeth Schröder, it is my honor to extend greetings on the occasion of the 775th anniversary of the church.

Grossmutter, at the age of 81, sent greetings on the occasion of your 700th anniversary in 1929. Seventy five years later, at the age of 93, I am deeply honored to be able to send these words on behalf of the Wiedow descendants now living in America. I live in Iowa, just a few miles from where Carl and Elisabeth eventually settled on their own farm and raised their family. By now you probably have seen pictures from that area: the house Grossvater built, the farmyard, the church that he helped build, and finally the gravestone at St. John's Cemetery where they were laid to rest.

We, the descendants of Carl and Elisabeth Wiedow, are pleased that Professor Knuth found us and connected us to the village and church of which Carl and Elisabeth were a part before they emigrated to this country. We are proud of our heritage.

Congratulations to you on this memorable occasion. May you have many more such celebrations!

*Harold Wiedow*

Fig. 14.5 Greetings sent by Harold Wiedow to the congregation at Eldena, Mecklenburg in July 2004 on the occasion of the 675-year celebration of the founding of the village.

Fig. 14.6  Float in parade held on the occasion of the 675-year celebration of the founding of Eldena.  Float depicts Carl Wiedow sailing to America. (Photo by E.L. Knuth, 2004)

# Chapter 15

# THE BREMERHAVEN EMIGRATION EXHIBIT

The success story of Carl Wiedow was featured in the emigration exhibit held in Bremerhaven, Germany in the summer of 2000 [16]. Bremerhaven was one of the most important emigration ports in Germany during the 19th and 20th centuries; about 7 million emigrants left from Bremerhaven for the USA. The opening ceremonies for the exhibit, "Abenteuer Spurensuche: Auswanderung nach Amerika," which translates into "An Adventure in the Footsteps of Emigrants to America," were held 2 June 2000, the day after the opening ceremonies for the world exposition, EXPO2000, in Hannover.

The invitation which my wife and I received quoted Swehn's letter from Iowa to his former teacher [1]: "Dear friend, you see that it has really become true _ _ _. We have plenty of everything: plenty land and plenty livestock. But it cost also plenty sweat." Since I had spent many years researching the true identity of Jürnjakob Swehn [17-21], we accepted the invitation with enthusiasm and anticipation.

Guests were greeted at the entrance (Fig. 15.1) by mannequins dressed in 19th century attire. The admission card, provided by Deutsche Telekom, was not only for admission but also (a) a key for operating computers which enabled personal interactions with the exhibit and (b) a Deutsche Telekom promotion in the form of a telephone card good for a nominal 3 DM of telephone time. The card was decorated with the photos of the prominent emigrants featured at the exhibit, namely Marlene Dietrich, Franz Daniel Pastorius, Rosa and Emil Scheuer, Carl Schurz, Justina Tubbe and Carl Wiedow, making the card also an attractive souvenir. (Fig. 15.2) The computer interactions guided the visitors through eight rooms, namely (1) The Emigrant, (2) The Childhood, (3) The Departure, (4) The Crossing (projected photos with commentary), (5) The New World, (6) The Death, (7) The Memories and (8) The End. The account which follows focuses on Carl Wiedow, AKA Jürnjakob Swehn. He is today one of the best-known immigrants from Germany to Iowa, having acquired instant recognition when it was found that he was the writer of many of the letters appearing in the Jürnjakob Swehn book.

In the first room, the visitors were greeted by life-sized likenesses of the emigrants embedded in otherwise-transparent cylindrical pillars. The photo of Carl Wiedow, used so prominently in the exhibit, was obviously from the Wiedow family photo (Fig. 3.5).

In the description of Carl Wiedow's early life in Glaisin, one learned that "Carl Wiedow hails from a desolate, barren region. The clay walls of the village huts are no match for the summer heat and winter wind. No one living here can lay claim to more than the bare essentials. But Carl has one advantage over his neighbors: he can read and write. When he emigrates to America to escape the poverty of his homeland, these skills will render him unforgettable to this day." This description concluded with a homespun quote from the book, "It's always good for a person to know where he's from."

Regarding his departure, the exhibit told that "Life is no bed of roses in Glaisin, a small town in Mecklenburg. While many villagers have at least secured their livelihoods through hereditary leaseholds on the prince's land, Carl has no option but to follow in his father's footsteps. Upon leaving school, he becomes a day laborer – the lot of many peasants in the region. But not everyone is willing to accept this cruel destiny: one after another, the people pack their meager belongings and head for America. Hoping to escape a life of poverty, the 19-year-old Carl joins them in 1868 [21]. He proceeds to the emigration center in the Port of Hamburg to await his steamship. At last the day of departure arrives and, convinced he will find good fortune in The New World, Carl puts out to sea. The date is July 20, 1868."

In the room titled "The New World," one found Carl Wiedow's life in America summarized in a brief paragraph. "His first steps in the New World bring him into New York's immigrant reception center. After leaving there, he survives by working at odd jobs. In 1872 he marries Catharina [22], with pet name Wieschen, who comes from his hometown, Glaisin. _ _ _ Carl works hard, saving every penny. By 1875 they had finally saved enough to buy their own farm in Clayton (sic), Iowa [23]. At first, the family lives cramped together in a small log cabin. But Carl is a skilled and experienced farmer and the farm begins to prosper. _ _ _ Carl Wiedow dies a wealthy farmer on November 19, 1913." The exhibit documented extensively the Wiedow family in Iowa via both pictures and records.

Perspective to the book, <u>Jürnjakob Swehn, der Amerikafahrer</u>, and to the role played by Carl Wiedow in the origin of the book, was provided by a quotation from H.K.A. Krüger [8]. Krüger, a close friend of Johannes

Gillhoff, asked him about the background of the book. Gillhoff answered, "My father was a teacher in Glaisin near Eldena. He lived there over fifty years and witnessed the era when emigration fever gripped the nation. Must have been 350 people that emigrated from Glaisin then to find a better life beyond the ocean. My father corresponded with half of them. That happened quite naturally. They wanted to hear about their old homeland, liked their teacher, and who else could they find to write to them? The ones who had stayed back, mostly old folk, were illiterate. Thus it was that the schoolmaster stepped in. One of the Wiedows, that I had christened Swehn, was the most avid correspondent." (The word christened is used figuratively here.) Photos of the gravestones of the several emigrants were featured in the room titled The Death. The photo of the Wiedow gravestone apparently was made in April 2000 specially for this exhibit.

Wiedow-family memories were provided in a video which was accessed via telephone using the Deutsche Telekom admission card. This video featured an interview with Harold Wiedow, grandson of Carl Wiedow. The memories recalled in this interview parallel those shared by Harold Wiedow with the present author in 1993 and with Nancy Willard, a granddaughter of Carl Wiedow, and published in the book, Cracked Corn and Snow Ice Cream [24]. We quote here from the book: "All the German people from this area came from Mecklenburg. Did you ever hear how Grossvater ran away and came to America? See, he and his buddy were going to be drafted into the Kaiser's army. So these two boys went to Hamburg and looked for a ship that was sailing to America, but there wasn't one leaving right away. They had to wait. One afternoon around the corner came two of the kaiser's soldiers. Those boys thought they'd be taken for sure. Now, the German women of that day wore very full skirts, and there was a woman sitting on the corner. She hid those boys under her skirt till the soldiers went by. Took them six weeks, but they got here." Regarding pioneer life in rural America, Harold recalled in the interview with Nancy that "If it hadn't been for your grandmother, my dad would have frozen to death. See, they walked home from St. John's school, four or five miles. The English River froze up solid, so they walked on the ice to get out of the wind. My dad wanted to lie down and go to sleep. Now, that's the last thing you should do in the cold. And your grandmother kept him a-going till she got him home."

The End of the exhibit summarized the presentation via printouts from an interactive computer. In Germany Carl Wiedow had been a day laborer. In Iowa, albeit with "plenty sweat," he reached his goal and was able to put his feet under his own kitchen table, live in his own house and farm his own land.

Fig. 15.1 Entrance to the exhibit, "An Adventure in the Footsteps of Emigrants to America," Bremerhaven, Germany, June 2, 2000. (Photo by E.L. Knuth, 2000)

Fig. 15.2 The admission card to the exhibit, "An Adventure in the Footsteps of Emigrants to America." The emigrants portrayed on the card (Franz Pastorius, Carl Wiedow, Justina Tubbe, Carl Schurz, Marlene Dietrich, Emil and Rosa Scheuer) are featured in the exhibit.

# Chapter 16

# UNEXPECTED HAPPENINGS

Particularly after I had identified the writer of the letters, my thoughts returned often to Johannes and his friend – to the Johannes from the Hotel Stadt Schwerin who had the courage to associate with a foreigner and to his friend who had grown up with the story of Jürnjakob Swehn. As I looked back on my researches, I saw that I was fortunately the right person at the right place at the right time. The combination of born in Clayton County, Iowa, roots in Mecklenburg, interest in genealogy, frequent visitor to Germany and ability to speak and read German was good fortune waiting to happen. But Johannes and his friend were the catalyst which activated the search. I wondered how they would react if they were to know what their comments had set in motion. I was convinced that the card which Johannes had given me in 1976 was somewhere in my study, and had looked for it many times without success. Then early in 2002, when I wasn't looking for it, I stumbled on it. (Fig. 16.1) It had been hiding almost 26 years in a book, "Schwerin, Skizzen aus einer alten Stadt" (Schwerin, Sketches from an old city), which I had bought during our brief visit to Schwerin in 1976.

After sharing my discovery with my wife, I went straight to my favorite telephone directory for Germany, teleauskunft.de, and in a few minutes had a list of three J. Lawrenz and five Johannes Lawrenz telephone numbers, but none of them in Schwerin. Two didn't answer – none of the other six was the correct one. Then I noticed a Restaurant Lukas, Inh. (Proprietor) Arne Lawrenz, in Schwerin. I called – success! Arne is a nephew of Johannes. Although Arne didn't have the phone number for Johannes, he assured me that his father did – gave me his father's phone number, and mentioned in passing that Johannes lives in Rodgau near Frankfurt. I didn't even need to call his father – I had noticed in the telephone listings a Johannes Löwenberg-Lawrenz in Rodgau but had been dissuaded from calling by the hyphenated name. The lady who answered assured me that I had reached the Johannes Lawrenz who was once employed in the Hotel Stadt Schwerin, indicated that Johannes was at the moment in Berlin on a business trip, gave me his cell-phone number and E-Mail address, and offered to have him return my call. We made telephone contact two days later. Johannes did not have a distinct recollection but confirmed that our contact at the hotel was typical of his behavior. He had been at odds with the East German government for some time, had made many contacts with foreigners and was in the habit of passing out his business card. His contacts with foreigners and his habit of passing out his business card had created even more problems for him. He finally was allowed to leave East Germany in 1983, settled in West Germany and published in 1984 his experiences in a five-part series in the West-German Stern Magazin. Subsequent articles appeared in the Reader's Digest and the Washington Post. The hyphenated name Löwenberg-Lawrenz came into being when he remarried. He was now an investment adviser. We wrote back and forth – I sent him a photo of my wife and myself taken during our 1976 visit to Schwerin. On the 13th of March he wrote that he recalled us clearly, that it was not he who had told us about the book, but that his friend, Wilfried Oeding, from Glaisin must have done so. I found it ironic that I had given talks in Glaisin annually since 1998, only a few blocks from where Oeding lives, and we had not met!

Back to teleauskunft.de. I found two Oedings – Wilfried and another who I learned later was Wilfried's son. From Wilfried's answering machine I got his cell-phone – and caught up with him while he was attending a lecture by Hartmut Brun. Small world! It was Hartmut Brun who, starting in 1998, had invited me to present my research findings at the Gillhoff Days, held annually in Glaisin. Wilfried was indeed surprised to learn what he had set in motion 26 years earlier!

A letter from Hartmut Brun arrived about the same time that the business card from Johannes surfaced. To my great surprise, Brun informed me that I would be receiving the Fritz Reuter Medal at the Gillhoff Days, to be held the 8th and 9th of June. I had never dreamed that the fun of answering, "Who wrote those letters?", would lead to such an honor. But he wrote that, for the moment, it was to be held in confidence. He asked also if I would say a few words at the traditional annual gathering at the graveside of Johannes Gillhoff. My attendance at the Gillhoff Days was no problem for me since I had already made arrangements to be at the Max Planck Institute in Göttingen for the entire month of June. Once the program for the Gillhoff Days appeared in print (March issue of the magazine Mecklenburg), I sent copies of the program to Johannes and Wilfried. We agreed to get together sometime during my stay in Germany.

Also in March, Udo Baarck wrote that he and the photographer Walter Hinghaus were arranging an exhibition dealing with emigration from Glaisin. It was to be held at the open-air Folklore Museum in Schwerin and had the enthusiastic support of Gesine Kröhnert, head of the museum. Hinghaus would exhibit some of the photos which he took in Iowa as part of the Jürnjakob Swehn Photo Project. Opening ceremonies would be held on the Sunday afternoon following the closing of the Gillhoff-Days program; my wife and I were invited to attend. The Gillhoff-Days weekend was beginning to look like a full weekend!

I asked Udo for advice on how to obtain a copy of the five-part series written by Johannes and published in Stern Magazin. He volunteered to request a copy for me through the library in Schwerin – and in mid-April I had a copy [25]. From the series I learned that, perhaps as a result of his wife's work as a free-lance photographer, Johannes had developed an interest in free-lance writing already before leaving East Germany. Hence the series describing his experiences leading up to his departure for West Germany was "a natural" for him.

The series describes both the events which led up to his disenchantment with East Germany and the arduous process required to leave East Germany legally. After he finished his compulsory two-year military service in 1972, and in order to enjoy preferential admission to a business school, he joined the Sozialistische Einheitspartei Deutschlands (Socialist Unity Party of Germany), which I will from now on call "the Party." The first friction between Johannes and the Party arose when he was taken out of an honors research group as a result of a perceived lack of loyalty to the party. Several months later he was reprimanded by the Party when he chose to study for final exams in Schwerin (rather in the school library) without party permission. At the end of the oral reprimand, Johannes lost his patience and threw his party book (a symbol of party membership) on the table. He was subsequently voted out of the Party and dismissed from the school. Since he needed a job and had gained experience as a waiter while he was a student, he took a job as a waiter at the Hotel Stadt Schwerin. He dreamed also that the experience might help him enter the restaurant business. He did well as a waiter and in June 1977 married a local girl. They lived first in an apartment building. But Johannes was not willing to tolerate the politically dominated monthly tenant meetings. For not attending the meetings, they were ostracized by the other tenants – who perhaps were afraid to associate with a dissenter. Johannes and his family then bought a rundown farmhouse outside of Schwerin and, through much hard work, brought it up to a comfort level which many East Germans would have envied. But Johannes was still not happy – he didn't like the compromises he had to make in order to become head waiter, and would like to have had the freedom to become a journalist. He did some free-lance writing for church publications for which his wife did free-lance photography. When he asked the Hotel for a leave to attend a church conference in Halle (also in East Germany), he got the impression that he would have to compromise himself in order to get the leave. He quit his job and a couple of days later, on the fifth of October 1982, Johannes and his wife submitted an application for departure to West Germany.

Even with persistence by Johannes and his wife, it took more than eight months to get a response. In the meantime, they supported themselves with free-lance work and by selling their furniture. Most of their friends in East Germany were afraid to associate with them and deserted them. The few friends which they had in West Germany provided them with moral support and with gifts. Their application was denied. They immediately submitted a second application. In October 1983, his wife was detained and her film confiscated. After she was released, they submitted a third application, this time including her detention as a further reason for leaving. In November, the state offered to let them go if they would submit a fourth application, this time omitting any mention of her detention. Finally, on the tenth of December 1983, more than fourteen months after their first application, they travelled from Schwerin to Hamburg. A most interesting story – entirely consistent with the Johannes which we had met in Hotel Stadt Schwerin in 1976!

Plans for the Gillhoff-Days weekend became more firm once I arrived in Göttingen at the end of May. Wilfried and I agreed to meet at his home on Friday evening but, due to a prior commitment to a youth soccer team, he would not be able to attend the Gillhoff-Days program. Johannes indicated that he had to be in Berlin that weekend, but that he definitely wanted to get together in Frankfurt the evening before we flew back to California. Rather unexpectedly, the invitation to attend the opening ceremonies of the exhibition in Schwerin on Sunday afternoon turned into an invitation to say a few words during the ceremonies.

The Friday evening with Wilfried (Fig. 16.2) was filled with reminiscing. Over beer, I detailed for him some of the Jürnjakob-Swehn activities which our chance meeting 26 years ago had set in motion; he shared with us some of his experiences in the context of the unification of the two Germanies. I showed him my Jürnjakob-Swehn photo album; he brought out the well-worn copy of the Swehn book which had been in the family since before he was born. I promised to send him replacement copies of the last several pages, which had disappeared already many years ago. At the end of an evening, the likes of which one does not experience very often, we parted with the warm hope that we would meet again during the weekend.

The annual gathering at the graveside of Johannes Gillhoff (in Ludwigslust) took place the next morning. (Fig. 16.3) My words of remembrance, chosen to be informative as well as laudatory, are included in Appendix G. My emphasis on the chapter, "At the Deathbed of my Mother," was motivated by the observation that some writers appeared to be unaware that this chapter was written by Johannes Gillhoff, although this detail is well documented [10].

After the traditional noonday Eintopf (hearty soup) at the Forsthof Restaurant in Glaisin and the traditional laying of flowers at the commemorative stone in front of the old schoolhouse where Gottlieb Gillhoff had taught, the guests congregated in the Kulturscheune (Culturebarn) for the awards ceremony. (The Kulturscheune began its life as a large half-timbered barnhouse but has been converted into a very attractive community center.) The 2002 Johannes Gillhoff Prize went to Kuno Karls, a writer from Hagenow, Mecklenburg. According to the program, the Fritz Reuter Medal was next. Instead, the Bürgermeister (Mayor), Jürgen Behrends, came to the podium, invited me to join him, and named me the first Ehrenbürger (honorary citizen) of Glaisin. (Fig. 16.4; also Appendix H) As I was voicing my surprise and "complaining" that my friends in Glaisin kept secrets very well, an old German saying came to me: "Aller guten Dinge sind drei" (All good things come in threes). I replied that I was proud to be a citizen of Glaisin – the village from which Jürnjakob Swehn had emigrated – the village which had won the most-beautiful-village award [26] – the village with the friendliest people in Germany!

Now the Fritz Reuter Medal was indeed next. (Fig. 16.5; also Appendix H) As part of my "acceptance speech," I acknowledged the role which Johannes and Wilfried had played 26 years previously. I explained that Wilfried had a prior commitment and I introduced his wife. As I explained also that Johnnes was in Berlin, a gentleman jumped up from the chair which I had vacated a few minutes previously and announced, "Ich bin doch hier!" (I am indeed here!) After 26 years, Johannes and I greeted each other again on-stage in Glaisin! (Fig. 16.6) A movie script couldn't have done it more dramatically. Johannes explained later that he had driven from Berlin that morning in order to be present and had just arrived as I was called to the stage. We continued our reunion during intermission and confirmed our plans to meet in Frankfurt the evening before my wife and I were scheduled to fly back to California.

Embedded in the opening ceremonies of the emigration exhibition the following afternoon was a get-together of old friends, including Walter Hinghaus, Udo Baarck, and Wilfried and Renate Oeding. (Fig. 16.7) After the ceremonies, Walter invited Margaret and me to his photo studio for an impromptu professional photo session. Our group congregated then in the Orangerie of the Schwerin Castle for a relaxing finish to a full and exciting weekend. (Fig. 16.8) Since the weekend included reunions with Wilfried and Johannes, an honorary citizenship, the Reuter Medal and introductory remarks at the exhibition opening, the weekend might be considered a fitting climax to a 26-year saga. It was Sunday the 9th of June 2002.

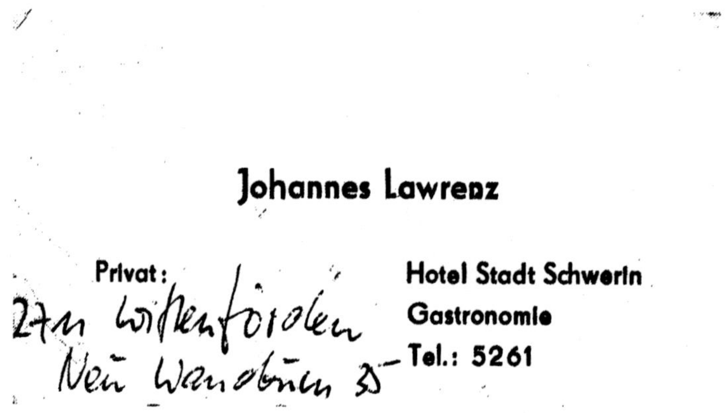

**Johannes Lawrenz**

Privat :                          Hotel Stadt Schwerin

*[handwritten address]*          Gastronomie

                                 Tel.: 5261

Fig. 16.1 The business card which Johannes Lawrenz gave me on June 12, 1976. The handwritten addition was his home address.

Fig. 16.2 Wilfried Oeding and the author on the occasion of their reunion 26 years after Oeding mentioned the Swehn book to the author. (Photo by M. Knuth, 2002)

Fig. 16.3 Words of remembrance at the graveside of Johannes Gillhoff. From left to right: Kuno Karls, Hartmut Brun, the author, Margaret Knuth, unidentified.

Fig. 16.4 Bürgermeister Jürgen Behrends welcoming the author as the first honorary citizen of Glaisin. (Photo by Kuno Karls, 2002)

Fig. 16.5 The author displaying the Fritz Reuter Medal which he has just received from Dr. Hartwig Bernitt, President of the Landsmannschaft Mecklenburg, standing to the left of the author. (Photo by M. Knuth, 2002)

Fig. 16.6 Johannes Lawrenz and the author on the occasion of their reunion 26 years after their first meeting in 1976 in Schwerin.

Fig. 16.7 The author (on left) and Photographer/Exhibitor Walter Hinghaus (on right) conversing with a guest at the emigration exhibition held at the open-air museum in Schwerin. (Photo by M. Knuth, 2002)

Fig. 16.8 Relaxing in the Orangerie Restaurant, Schwerin Castle, at the end of the Gillhoff-Days weekend. From left to right: Carol Madsen (descendant of the Wiedow family from Liepe), Katja Braun, Udo Baarck, Rüdiger Landt, Wilfried Oeding. (Photo by M. Knuth, 2002)

# ACKNOWLEDGEMENTS

Very special appreciation is due Mrs. Myra Voss, Clayton Co. Genealogist and special friend. Her assistance in locating relevant Clayton Co. church records and in contacting living descendants of the Charly Wiedow family was invaluable. For those questions in which also she came to a dead end (e.g., the date and place of death of Carl Wiedow's mother), I believe it nearly certain that the answer does not exist in Clayton Co.

Valuable assistance in locating material relevant to the Wiedow family in Iowa County was provided by Netha Meyer of the Iowa County Genealogy Society and the Iowa County Resource Library; also by Ferne Norris and Velma James of the Poweshiek County Historical and Genealogical Society. Dorothy Davis, a descendant of Johann Roesch and Carolina Schütt, provided extensive information regarding the Roesch-Schütt family. The letters in Chapter 4 were provided by Larry Rösch, the letters in Appendix E by Bill and Ruth Jahlas.

Special thanks are due also to the late Franz Schubert and the late Dr. Günther Schröder of Göttingen for sharing with me literature regarding Jürnjakob Swehn and his author, Johannes Gillhoff. Udo Baarck, member of the Johannes Gillhoff Society in Glaisin, was always ready and willing to provide copies of records from the archives in Schwerin. For help with sorting and correlating the data under the several variations of the Wiedow name, I am grateful to Rolf Gödecke (Hamburg) and Friedrich-Wilhelm Witt (Radolfzell am Bodensee), both of whom have close ties to Mecklenburg.

The hospitality and assistance of those descendants of Carl Wiedow (Harold Wiedow; the late Alice Wolf, nee Wiedow; Sharon McKay, nee Wolf; Bill Nyweide, grandson of Bertha Wiedow; Wm. M. Welch, son-in-law of Henry Wiedow; Wm. W. Welch, grandson of Henry Wiedow, and Susan Wehmeier, granddaughter of Mame Wiedow) with whom I have been in contact is appreciated greatly. They enriched this publication with oral family history and with photos.

My wife's companionship and willingness to accompany me in numerous "side trips" and visits during the two decades of researches summarized here are valued greatly.

# LITERATURE AND NOTES

1. Johannes Gillhoff, Jürnjakob Swehn, der Amerikafahrer. München: Deutscher Taschenbuch Verlag, 1978.

2. Johannes Gillhoff, Letters of a German American Farmer (translated by Richard L.A. Trost). Iowa City: University of Iowa Press, 2000.

3. Gravestone of Gottlieb Gillhoff, located in a field on outskirts of Glaisin, Mecklenburg.

4. Gravestone of Johannes Gillhoff, cemetery in Ludwigslust, Mecklenburg

5. Hartmut Brun, "Wiedow oder Jalass." Schwerin:Norddeutscher Leuchtturm (Beil. der Norddeutschen Zeitung), 23.05.1986

6. Joachim Reppmann, "Jürnjakob Swehn Symposium." Northfield, MN: Society for German-American Studies Newsletter, September 1993.

7. H. Otto Weltzien, "Jürnjakob Swehn und sein Verfasser." Bremen: Niedersachsen, 23:132, 1917/1918.

8. Werner Schnoor, "Auf den Spuren des Jürnjakob Swehn." Schwerin: Mecklenburgische Kirchenzeitung, 21.08.1977.

9. Hartmut Brun, Johannes Gillhoff, ein Lesebuch. Rostock: Hinstorf Verlag, 1988.

10. H.K.A. Krüger, "Aus Johannes Gillhoffs letztem Jahr." Rostock: Mecklenburgische Monatshefte, 6:130-133, 1930.

11. Johannes and Theodor Gillhoff, Möne Markow, der neue Amerikafahrer. München: Deutscher Taschenbuch Verlag, 1989.

12. Dieter Rakow, "Jürnjakob Swehn und seine Farm in Iowa," Mecklenburg, 44, No. 3, pp. 14-15, 2002.

13. E.L. Knuth, "Carl Wiedow und seine Farm in Iowa," Mecklenburg, 45, No. 6, pp. 14-15, 2003.

14. Arthur P. Rose, "An Illustrated History of Nobles County, Minnesota." Worthington, MN: Northern History Publishing Co., 1908.

15. E.L. Knuth, "The Johannes Gillhoff Society." Northfield, MN: Society for German-American Studies Newsletter, September 1999.

16. E.L. Knuth, "An Adventure in the Footsteps of Emigrants to America," Hawkeye Heritage, Winter 2000, pp. 179-183.

17. E.L. Knuth, "Jürnjakob Swehn, Emigrant to America," Hawkeye Heritage, Winter 1997, pp. 229-240.

18. E.L. Knuth, "Jürnjakob Swehn war doch ein Wiedow," Mecklenburg, 40, No. 3, pp. 20-21 and No. 4, p. 20, 1998.

19. E.L. Knuth, "Jürnjakob Swehn: the Continuing Story," Hawkeye Heritage, Fall 1999, pp. 141-144.

20. E.L. Knuth, "Wer war Jürnjakob Swehn?" Kikut, 24, pp. 57-67. Stavenhagen: Fritz- Reuter-Literaturmuseum, 2003. Also Johannes-Gillhoff-Jahrbuch, 2004, pp. 43-49. Rostock: MV Taschenbuch, 2004.

21. E.L. Knuth, "Auf den Spuren von Carl Wiedows Eltern und Geschwistern, Johannes-Gillhoff-Jahrbuch, 2004, pp. 54-60. Rostock: MV Taschenbuch, 2004.

22. According to his birth record, Carl Wiedow was in reality 20 years of age at the time he left Mecklenburg; both the book and the Wiedow family agree that Carl crossed on a sailship rather than on a steamship.

23. The exhibit uses the name Catharina, the first name given to her at baptism. In Iowa, she used Elisabeth, the second of her three given names.

24. While living in Clayton County, Carl and Elisabeth apparently rented a farm. Iowa County records show that Carl acquired the deed to 80 acres in Iowa County on 29 December 1884.

25. Nancy Willard and Jane Dyer, <u>Cracked Corn and Snow Ice Cream</u>. New York: Harcourt Brace and Co., 1997.

26. Johannes Lawrenz, a five-part series in <u>Stern Magazin</u>, 1984.
    "Ich will raus" (I want out) Vol. 15, pp. 64-76, April 5.
    "Wem kann man noch trauen?" (Who can one still trust?) Vol. 16, pp. 66-74, April 12.
    "Wehe dem, der aus der Reihe tanzt" (Woe to him, who dances out of line) Vol. 17, pp. 76-88, April 18.
    "Die Ablehnung" (The Rejection) Vol. 18, pp. 90-98, April 26.
    "Am Ende eines langen Weges" (At the End of a long Path) Vol. 19, pp. 88-96, May 3.

27. Glaisin won the Mecklenburg-Vorpommern competition "Our Village will become more beautiful – our village has a future" in 1998 and a similar national competition in 1999.

# PRIMARY DATA SOURCES

1. Church records from Mecklenburg: Conow, Dömitz, Eldena, Gorlosen, Grabow, Gross Laasch, Gross Pankow and Muchow
2. Church records from Brandenburg: Berge
3. Consent to emigrate: Schröder family from Glaisin, dated 11 August 1868.
4. Release from military service: Johann Carl Friedrich Wiedow, dated 16 March 1870.
5. Consent to emigrate: Johann Joachim Friedrich Wiede, his wife (nee Jarmer), and children Johann Carl Heinrich and Anna Marie Elisabeth, dated 26 March 1870.
6. Agent list: Johann Joachim Friedrich Wiede, Maria (nee Jarmer), Johann Carl Heinrich and Anna Marie Elisabeth, scheduled to sail 15 April 1870.
7. Passenger lists
    (a) Weser, arrived in N.Y. 5 Oct. 1867.
    (b) Saxonia, arrived in N.Y. 21 May 1868.
    (c) Hammonia, arrived in N.Y. 23 May 1868.
    (d) Germania, arrived in N.Y. 15 Oct. 1868.
    (e) Friedenburg, arrived in N.Y. 31 May 1870.
8. U.S. Census, 1870.
    (a) Garnavillo Twp, Clayton Co., Iowa.
    (b) Read Twp, Clayton Co., Iowa
    (c) Volga Twp, Clayton Co., Iowa
9. U.S. Census, 1880.
    (a) Giard Twp, Clayton Co., Iowa
    (b) Grand Meadow Twp, Clayton Co., Iowa.
    (c) Read Twp, Clayton Co., Iowa.
    (d) Volga Twp, Clayton Co., Iowa.
    (e) Hartford Twp, Iowa Co., Iowa.
10. U.S. Census, 1900.
    (a) Read Twp, Clayton Co., Iowa.
    (b) Lincoln Twp, Iowa Co., Iowa
    (c) Hartford Twp, Iowa Co., Iowa.
    (d) Deep River Twp, Poweshiek Co., Iowa
    (e) Saratoga Twp, Howard Co., Iowa

11. U.S. Census, 1910.
    (a) Garnavillo Twp, Clayton Co., Iowa
    (b) Lincoln Twp, Iowa Co., Iowa.
    (c) Deep River Twp, Poweshiek Co., Iowa
12. U.S. Census, 1920.
    (a) Lincoln Twp, Iowa Co., Iowa.
    (b) Deep River Twp, Poweshiek Co., Iowa
    (c) City of Muscatine, Muscatine Co., Iowa
13. Iowa Census, 1885.
    (a) Giard Twp, Clayton Co., Iowa
    (b) Hartford Twp, Iowa Co., Iowa
    (c) Lincoln Twp, Iowa Co., Iowa.
14. Iowa Census, 1895.
    (a) Giard Twp, Clayton Co., Iowa
    (b) Hartford Twp, Iowa Co., Iowa
    (c) Lincoln Twp, Iowa Co., Iowa.
15. Iowa Census, 1905. Saratoga Twp, Howard Co., Iowa.
16. Iowa Census, 1925. Deep River Twp, Poweshiek Co., Iowa
17. St. Paul Lutheran Church, Garnavillo, Iowa.
    (a) Marriage, Ahrends-Schröder, 22 Oct 1868.
    (b) Marriage, Wiedow-Schröder, 16 Mar 1872.
    (c) Birth, Heinrich Wiedow, 5 Jan 1873.
    (d) Birth, Maria Wiedow, 25 Aug 1874.
    (e) Marriage, Wiedow-Müller, 29 March 1875.
    (f) Death, Johann Schröder, 15 Mar 1882.
    (g) Death, Karl Ahrends, 22 Aug. 1922.
18. Zion Lutheran Church, Clayton Center, Iowa.
    (a) Marriage, Schrank-Wiedow, 14 March 1873.
    (b) Death, Heinrich Schrank, 3 May 1875.
    (c) Marriage, Schuldt-Wiedow, 16 July 1875.
    (d) Birth, Elise Dorethea Marie Wiedow, 31 Oct 1879.
    (e) Marriage, Wiedow-Schroth, 21 Feb. 1881.
19. St. Paul Lutheran Church, Postville, Iowa.
    Burial, Wilhelmine Wiedow, 15 Jan. 1880.
20. St. John's Evangelical Lutheran Church, Victor, Iowa.
    (a) Communion, Carl and Elisabeth Wiedow, 3 Jul 1881.
    (b) Birth, Karl Heinrich Wilhelm Wiedow, 18 Sep 1884.
    (c) Death, Jochim Wiedow, 19 Jan 1888.
    (d) Birth, Bertha Caroline Wiedow, 22 Feb 1889.
    (e) Confirmation, Maria Wiedow, 30 March 1890.
    (f) Confirmation, Elise Dorothea Maria Wiedow, 1895.

(g) Death, Johann Joachim Jalass, 27 Jul 1895.

(h) Confirmation, Karl Heinrich Wilhelm Wiedow, 1899.

(i) Marriage, Shepperd-Wiedow, 1 Jan 1901.

(j) Death, Maria (nee Rösch) Schröder, 30 Mar 1903.

(k) Confirmation, Bertha Caroline Wiedow, 5 Apr 1903.

(l) Death, Maria (nee Schroth) Wiedow, 9 Oct. 1903.

(m) Marriage, Nyweide-Wiedow, 28 Nov 1912.

(n) Death, Carl Wiedow, 19 Nov 1913.

(o) Death, Elisabeth (nee Schröder) Wiedow, 16 Oct 1930.

21. Immanuel Lutheran Church, Elkport, Iowa
    Marriage, Schröder-Barthels, 9 Jan. 1878.

22. Clayton Co. Civil Records, Elkader, Iowa
    (a) Marriage, Schult-Schröder, 20 Aug 1868.
    (b) Marriage, Ahrends-Schröder, 21 Oct 1868.
    (c) Citizenship Application, Carl Wiedow, 11 March 1872.
    (d) Marriage, Wiedow-Schröder, 16 March 1872.
    (e) Marriage, Schuldt-Wiedow, 14 March 1873.
    (f) Marriage, Wiedow-Müller, 29 March 1875.
    (g) Marriage, Wiedow-Schroth, 21 Feb. 1881.

23. Iowa Co. Civil Records, Marengo, Iowa
    Death, Carl Wiedow, 19 Nov 1913.
    Record of deed filing, 5 Jan. 1885.

24. Atlas of Iowa County, Iowa. Mason City, Iowa: Anderson Publishing Co., 1917. See Lincoln Twp.

25. College of Medicine, University of Iowa, Iowa City, Iowa. Transcript of records, Henry Wiedow, 1902.

26. Obituary, Carl Wiedow, The Victor Record, Victor, Iowa, 26 Nov 1913.

27. Obituary, Mrs. Elisabeth Wiedow, 1930.

28. Obituary, Dr. Henry Wiedow, The Desert Trail, Twenty Nine Palms, California, 20 Dec 1940.
    Obituary, Dr. Henry Wiedow, The Deep River Record, Deep River, Iowa, 26 Dec 1940.

29. Obituary, Mrs. C.L. Sheppard.
    Obituary, Dr. Cary Sheppard, Owosso Argus Press, Owosso, Michigan, 23 Apr 1959.

30. Obituary, Mrs. Louis C. Furney, Williamsburg Journal Tribune, Williamsburg, Iowa, 7 Aug 1913.

31. Obituary, Charles Wiedow, 1966.
    Obituary, Velda (nee Forney) Wiedow, 1989.

32. Burial records, Greenwood Cemetery, Muscatine, Iowa.

Henry Nyweide

Bertha (nee Wiedow) Nyweide

33. Obituary, Elsie Josephine (nee Prashak) Wiedow, 1999.

34. Obituary, Alice (nee Wiedow) Wolf, 2002.

35. Obituary, Dr. Hobart H. Willard, 7 May 1974.

36. Obituary, Prof. Robert R. Korfhage, Pittsburgh Post-Gazette, 22 Nov. 1998.

37. Obituary, Clark T. Wiedow, Newton Daily News, 5 March 2004.

38. Letter from Gottlieb Gillhoff to his cousin, Carolina (nee Schütt) Rösch, 28 Feb. 1890.

39. Letter from Gottlieb Gillhoff to his cousin, Carolina (nee Schütt) Rösch, 22 Aug. 1907.

40. Letter from Theo. Gillhoff to Pastor Wm. F. Ullerich, Victor, Iowa, 3 Nov. 1920.

41. Letter from Theo. Gillhoff to the Jahlas family, 10 Jan. 1923.

42. Letter from Theo. Gillhoff to the Jahlas family, 31 Dec. 1924.

43. Letter from Edythe Wiedow (adopted daughter of Henry and Cora Wiedow) to her Aunt Bertha (nee Wiedow) Nyweide, 29 Dec 1940.

44. Letter from Edythe Wiedow to Sharon McKay (great granddaughter of Carl and Elisabeth Wiedow), 9 Jun 1990.

# Appendix A

# WIEDOW GENEALOGY CHARTS

The relatively extensive data pertaining to the genealogy of the Wiedow family which is the subject of this book is summarized here in two charts – an Ahnentafel Chart (family tree) for Heinrich Wiedow, the oldest son of Carl Wiedow (AKA Jürnjakob Swehn) and Elisabeth Schröder (AKA Wieschen) and a Descendancy Chart for Ernst Joachim Christian Wiede, great-grandfather of Carl Wiedow. Although I have not yet searched for them, it is likely that descendants of the siblings of Carl Wiedow's father are living somewhere in Mecklenburg. And although data for more recent generations is available, I have terminated the Descendancy Chart at five generations in order to protect the privacy of living descendants. In the Ahnentafel Chart one finds the abbreviations b (birth), c (christening), m (married), d (death), b (burial), Abt (about) and Bef (before); also the German occupational terms Tageloehner (day laborer), Haeusler (worker in a cottage industry), Kuhhirte (cowherder), Hauswirth (landlord), Knecht (farm-hand), Huetmann (herdsman), Buedner (worker in a cottage industry), Hirte (herdsman), Schulze (mayor), Krueger (innkeeper), Schiffsknecht (ship-hand), Halbhuefner (owner of a small farm), Ochsenknecht (oxen-hand), Zimmermeister (master carpenter), Einlieger (resident), Schmied (blacksmith), Hausmann (caretaker) and Steuermann (helmsman).

A Descendancy Chart for Hans Jochim Roesch also is included here in order to help clarify the relationship between Carolina Schütt (Gottlieb Gillhoff's cousin) and Elisabeth Schröder (AKA Wieschen). I have terminated this chart at four genrations in order to simplify the chart, keeping in mind its purpose. Note that Elisabeth Schröder's mother, Maria Elisabeth Dorothea Roesch, was a sister of Johann Jürgen Heinrich Roesch, husband of Carolina Schütt. In Iowa County, the Wiedow-Schröder family and the Roesch-Schütt families were neighbors. Letters from the Wiedow-Schröder family to the schoolteacher are included in the Jürnjakob Swehn book [1,2]; letters from the schoolteacher to the Roesch-Schütt family are presented in Chapter 4 of the present book.

## 1st GENERATION

1 Heinrich Wiedow [Dr.]: b 5 Jan 1873 Garnavillo,Iowa; m 4 Jul 1899 ; d 17 Dec 1940 Twenty Nine Palms,CA

## 2nd GENERATION

2 Carl Friederich Johann Wiedow [Juernjakob Swehn]: b 8 Nov 1847 Bellevue; m 16 Mar 1872 Garnavillo,Iowa; d
  19 Nov 1913 Lincoln Twp,Iowa Co
3 Catharina Elisa Johanna Schroeder: b 29 Sep 1847 Glaisin; d 16 Oct 1930 Muscatine,Iowa

## 3rd GENERATION

4 Johan Joachim Friederich Wiedow [Tageloehner]: b 25 Apr 1817 Suelze; m 15 Jun 1847 Grabow; d 19 Jan 1888
  Lincoln Twp,Iowa Co
5 Maria Sophia Catharina Elisabeth Jarmer: b 23 Dec 1822 Muddelmasch
6 Johann Jochim Heinrich Schroeder [Haensler]: b 15 May 1810 Glaisin; m 11 Feb 1842 Eldena; d 15 Mar 1882
  Farmersburg,Iowa
7 Maria Elisabeth Dorothea Roesch: b 14 Jun 1821 Glaisin; d 30 Mar 1903 Lincoln Twp,Iowa Co,Iowa

## 4th GENERATION

8 Johann Ernst Joachim Christoph Wiedow (Wiede/Wiese) [Tageloehner]: b 25 Sep 1777 Kleeste; m 15 Oct 1803
  Gross Pankow; d 16 Jan 1821 Gross Pankow
9 Anna Ilsabe [Marie] Harm: b 5 Mar 1779 Gross Pankow
10 Johann Friedrich Christian Jarmer [Kuhhirte]: b 24 Sep 1797 Muddelmasch; m 25 Jan 1822 Gross Laasch
11 Augusta Christina Johanna Springer: b 13 Mar 1797 Kolbow; d 18 Jan 1837 Neu Karstaedt
12 Daniel Hinrich Schroeder [Hauswirth]: b 1755/1759 Goehren; m 29 Nov 1796 Eldena; d 24 Nov 1832 Glaisin
13 Anna Maria Moeller: b 1777 Goehren
14 Johann Jochim Roesch [Knecht]: c 28 May 1783 Eldena; m 9 Feb 1819 Eldena; d 6 Sep 1838 Glaisin
15 Maria Elisabeth Dorothea Boeckman: b 24 Sep 1792 Karenz; d 8 Aug 1822 Glaisin

## 5th GENERATION

16 Ernst Joachim Christian Wiede [Huetmann]
17 Margaretha Elisabeth Dorothea Brahn
18 Christopher Harm [Hauswirth]: c 6 May 1735 Gross Pankow; m 22 Nov 1776 Gross Pankow
19 Catharina Maria Schult: c 18 Jan 1753 Gross Pankow
20 Christian Friederich Jarmer [Buedner]: b 6 Aug 1756 Carstaedt; m 18 Nov 1783 Gross Laasch; d 5 Mar 1814
   Muddelmasch
21 Sophia Elisabeth Koeper: b Abt 1760 Dadow
22 Johann Friedrich Springer [Hirte]: b Abt 1762 Boeck; m 2 Oct 1788 Gorlosen; d 13 May 1832 Eldena
23 Ilsabe Maria Meier: b 19 Oct 1761 Gross Laasch; d 5 Jan 1811 Eldena
24 Christian Schroeder [Schulze]: b Abt 1718 ; d May 1784 Goehren
25 Maria Ilsabe Ludemann: b Abt 1728 ; d 8 Apr 1797 Goehren
26 Peter Adolph Moeller [Hauswirth]
27 Catharina Maria Timm
28 Hans Jochim Roesch [Tageloehner]: d Bef 1819
29 Maria Elisabeth Mundt: b 1752 Straas; d 28 May 1831 Glaisin
30 Jochim Hinrich Boeckman [Tageloehner]: c 21 Nov 1764 Conow; m 15 Nov 1791 Conow; d 3 Apr 1840 Karenz
31 Marie Liese Dorothea Sass: c 16 May 1764 Conow

## 6th GENERATION

36 Jochim Harm: c 26 Sep 1689 Gross Pankow; m 14 Nov 1726 Gross Pankow
37 Catharina Harms
38 Christopher Schult: c 6 Oct 1713 Gross Pankow; m 2 Nov 1753 Gross Pankow; bu 14 Sep 1762 Gross Pankow

143

39 Margarethe Elisabeth Gronow
40 Johann Juergen Jarmer [Krueger]: b Karstaedt; m 14 Jul 1751  Gross Laasch
41 Catharina Margarethe Beencke: b Abt 1726  Karstaedt?; d 7 Jan 1786  Karstaedt
42 Johann David Koeper [Kuhhirte]: c 16 Nov 1732  Grabow; d 5 Dec 1787  Dadow
43 M. Graf: b Abt 1735 ; d 14 Jan 1795  Dadow
44 Johan Ludwig Springer: d Bef 1811
46 Peter Zarnck [Hauswirth]
47 Anna Margaretha Meier
48 Adolph Schroeder [Schulze]
52 Jochim Diederich Moeller
60 Adam Boeckman [Schiffsknecht]: b Moellenbeck?; m 2 Dec 1755  Conow
61 Sophia Elisabeth Mau: b 8 Jul 1733  Carentz
62 Caspar Friedrich Sass: b 2 Sep 1738  Conow; m 23 Nov 1762  Conow
63 Anna Maria Schult: b 6 Jan 1739  Grebs

## 7th GENERATION

72 Gabriel Harm: m 1687 ; Gross Pankow
73 Liese Camin
76 Jochim Schult [Hauswirth]
82 Hans Jochim Beencke [Halbhuefner]
84 Hans Jochim (Juergen) Koeper [Ochsenknecht]: c 26 Oct 1697  Grabow; m 8 Nov 1725  Grabow
85 Anna Dorothea Zohm: c 18 May 1696  Grabow
120 Adam Boeckman: d Bef 1755
122 Jochen Ulrich Mau [Zimmermeister]: b Karenz?; m 2 Nov 1723  Conow
123 Ilsabe Geister: c 29 Sep 1695  Conow
124 Jochim Sass [Hauswirth]: c 1 Dec 1692  Conow; m 26 Jun 1725  Conow; bu 13 Nov 1768  Conow
125 Trinn Greth Meier: c 29 Jul 1702  Conow
126 Hans Christopher Schult [Einlieger]: b Feb 1707  Rattenfort; m 30 Nov 1734  Conow
127 Maria Elisabeth Schultz: b Mar 1712  Schlesien

## 8th GENERATION

168 Jochim Koepe [Kuhhirte]: c 27 Sep 1654  Grabow; m 19 Apr 1692  Grabow; d 1698  Bekenthin
169 Anna Maria Vielhaken: c 27 Dec 1668  Grabow
170 Jochim Zohm [Jr.]: b Cremmin?; m 13 Nov 1673  Grabow
171 Lisebeth Ratsack: c 10 Dec 1656  Grabow
246 Jochim Geister [Hauswirth]: b Carentz?
247 Ann
248 Marten Sass [Kuhhirte]: b Conow?
249 Trien
250 Johann Meier [Hauswirth]: m 15 Nov 1692 ; Conow
251 Elisabeth Teess: b Glaisin
252 Johann Schult: b Rattenfort; m 14 Mar 1700  Conow
253 Lehn Gret Koetter: b Rattenfort?
254 Hans Christopher Schultz: m 30 Jul 1709 ; Conow
255 Anna Maria Dasse

## 9th GENERATION

336 Juergen Grantz
337 Elst Koeppe
338 Jochim Vielhaken
339 Anna Rodatz
340 Jochim Zohm
341 Liesebeth

144

342 Jacob Ratsack [Schmied]: b Cremmin?; m  1 Dec 1652  Grabow
343 Trinn Bastian
492 Joch. Geister [Hauswirth]
500 Casten Meier [Hausmann]
502 Peter Teess [Schultze]: d Bef 1703
508 Caspar Schultz
510 Hans Dasse [Steuermann]

## 10th GENERATION

672 Juergen Grantz

| Name | (Birth/Chr.-Death/Burial) | Birth/Chr. Place |
|------|---------------------------|------------------|

```
1-- Ernst Joachim Christian Wiede [Huetmann] (   -    )
sp-Margaretha Elisabeth Dorothea Brahn (   -    )
    2-- Catharina Maria Wiede (1773-   )  Kleeste
    2-- Ilse Catharina Margarethe Wiede (1775-   )  Kleeste
    2-- Johann Ernst Joachim Christoph Wiedow (Wiede/Wiese) [Tageloehner] (1777-1821)  Kleeste
    sp-Anna Ilsabe (Marie) Harm (1779-   )  Gross Pankow
        3-- Johann Jochim Heinrich Wiedow (1804-1847)  Panckow
        sp-Auguste Elisabeth Henrica Carolina Peters (1805-   )  Eldena
        3-- Jacob Friederich Wiede (1807-   )  Gross Pankow
        3-- Carl David Wiedow (1809-   )  Beckentin
        3-- Joachim Friederich Moritz Wiedow (1812-   )  Gueritz
        3-- Johanna Marie Sophia Wiedow (1815-1816)  Gueritz
        3-- Johan Joachim Friederich Wiedow [Tageloehner] (1817-1888)  Suelze
        sp-Maria Sophia Catharina Elisabeth Jarmer (1822-   )  Muddelmasch
            4-- Carl Friederich Johann Wiedow [Juernjakob Swehn] (1847-1913)  Bellevue
            sp-Catharina Elisa Johanna Schroeder (1847-1930)  Glaisin
                5-- Heinrich Wiedow [Dr.] (1873-1940)  Garnavillo,Iowa
                sp-Cora Simpson (1869-1928)
                5-- Maria Wiedow (1874-1956)  Garnavillo,Iowa
                sp-Cary Lowe Sheppard [Osteopath] (1872-1959)  Mt. Pleasant,Pa
                5-- Elise Dorethea Marie Wiedow (1879-1911)  Read Twp,Clayton Co,Iowa
                sp-Louis Cameron Forney [Carpenter] (1874-1955)  Dayton Twp,Iowa County
                5-- Karl Heinrich Wilhelm Wiedow [Cabinet Maker] (1884-1966)  Lincoln Twp,Iowa Co,Iowa
                sp-Velda Lenore Forney (1890-1989)  Deep River,IA
                5-- Bertha Caroline Wiedow (1889-1973)  Lincoln Twp,Iowa Co,Iowa
                sp-Henry J. Nyweide [Driver] (1882-1945)  Holland
            4-- Johann Carl Friederich Wiedow [Farmer] (1851-1930)  Bellevue
            sp-Wilhelmine Mueller (1855-1880)  Stolp,Pommern
                5-- Wilhelmine Caroline Margarethe Wiedow (1876-1949)  Read Twp,Clayton Co
                sp-Asa C. Wilmont (   -    )
                sp-Oscar J. Tyrrell (   -    )
            sp-Anna Maria Schroth (1855-1903)  Wuertemberg
                5-- Maria Henrietta Wiedow (1881-1929)  Littleport,Iowa
                sp-Carl H. Timm (   -    )
                5-- Adolph Heinrich Carl Wiedow (1882-1956)  Victor,Iowa
                5-- Catharina Barbara Wiedow (1887-   )  Victor,Iowa
                5-- Johann Friedrich Emil Wiedow (1889-1968)  Victor,Iowa
            4-- Anna Maria Elisabeth Wiedow (1853-   )  Glaisin
            sp-Heinrich Schrank (1853-1875)
                5-- Wilhelmine Henrietta Margarethe Schrank (1874-   )  Farmersburg Twp,IA
            sp-Johann Juergen Heinrich Schuldt (1837-   )  Gross Schmoelen
                5-- Marie Louise Schuldt (1876-   )  Giard Twp,Clayton County,Iowa
                5-- Anna Dorethea Elise Schuldt (1878-   )  Giard Twp,Clayton County,IA
                5-- Heinrich Carl Schuldt (1880-   )  Giard Twp,Clayton County,IA
                5-- Carl Johann Heinrich Schuldt (1882-   )  Giard Twp,Clayton County,IA
                5-- Wilhelm Heinrich Christoph Schuldt (1884-   )  Giard Twp,Clayton County,IA
                5-- Hermann Christoph Louis Schuldt (1887-   )  Giard Twp,Clayton County,IA
                5-- Johann Joachim Schuldt (1889-   )  Giard Twp,Clayton County,IA
                5-- Eddi Friederich Wilhelm Carl Schuldt (1892-   )  Giard Twp,Clayton County,IA
                5-- Alvine Charlotte Mathilde Elise Schuldt (1896-   )  Giard Twp,Clayton County,IA
    2-- Friedrich Ludwig Wiede (1779-1780)  Kleeste
    2-- Friedrich Ludwig Wiede (1781-   )  Klein Berge
```

146

| Name | (Birth/Chr.-Death/Burial) | Birth/Chr. Place |
|------|---------------------------|------------------|

```
1-- Hans Jochim Roesch [Tageloehner] (    -1819)
 sp-Maria Elisabeth Wundt (1752-1831)  Straas
    2-- Maria Elisabeth Roesch (1781-1781)  Eldena
    2-- Catharina Maria Roesch (1782-   )  Eldena
    2-- Johann Jochim Roesch [Knecht] (1783-1838)  Eldena
     sp-Maria Elisabeth Dorothea Boeckman (1792-1822)  Karenz
        3-- Carolina Anna Maria Roesch (1815-   )  Glaisin
        3-- Maria Elisabeth Dorothea Roesch (1821-1903)  Glaisin
         sp-Johann Jochim Heinrich Schroeder [Haeusler] (1810-1882)  Glaisin
            4-- Elisabeth Maria Catharina Johanna Schroeder (1842-   )  Glaisin
             sp-Karl Ahrend (   -   )
            4-- Elisa Maria Dorothea Wilhelmine Schroeder (1845-   )  Glaisin
             sp-Johann Juergen Heinrich Schultz (   -   )
            4-- Catharina Elisa Johanna Schroeder (1847-1930)  Glaisin
             sp-Carl Friederich Johann Wiedow [Juernjakob Swehn] (1847-1913)  Bellevue
            4-- Johann Jochim Christian Daniel Schroeder (1849-1927)  Glaisin
             sp-Maria Bartels (1851-   )
            4-- Sophia Catharina Johanna Schroeder (1852-1853)  Glaisin
            4-- Catharina Elisa Wilhelmina Schroeder (1860-1860)  Glaisin
            4-- Joachim Carl Heinrich Schroeder (1863-1863)  Glaisin
            4-- Christian Carl Jacob Schroeder (1863-1863)  Glaisin
        3-- Catharina Elisabeth Henrica Roesch (1825-   )  Glaisin
        3-- Johann Heinrich Christian Roesch (1827-   )  Glaisin
        3-- Johann Juergen Heinrich Roesch (1831-1895)  Glaisin
         sp-Carolina Maria Dorothea Lucia Schuett (1838-1921)  Glaisin
    2-- Stillbirth Roesch (1786-1786)  Glaisin
    2-- Ana Dorothea Roesch (1787-1790)  Glaisin
    2-- Ana Margaretha Roesch (1789-1790)  Glaisin
    2-- Helena Catharina Roesch (1792-   )  Glaisin
```

147

# Appendix B

# BIOGRAPHY, DR. HENRY WIEDOW

The biography which follows is from <u>An Illustrated History of Nobles County, Minnesota</u> [14], a copy of which is in the possession of the Nobles County Historical Society, Worthington, MN. The biography was found, copied and sent to me by Carol Madsen, a descendant of the Wiedow family from Liepe (Appendix F). Since it probably was either written by or approved by Dr. Wiedow, I take it to be more reliable than details handed down orally within the family or recalled in his obituaries.

"Dr. Henry Wiedow, physician and surgeon of Worthington, was born in Clayton County, Iowa, January 5, 1873, the son of Charles and Elizabeth (Schroeder) Wiedow. Both parents were born in Germany, came to the United States in their youth, and were married in this country. The first twenty years of the life of our subject were spent on a farm. He then matriculated in the Marengo, Iowa High School, from which school he was graduated in 1897. After a two years' academic course in the University of Iowa, Henry Wiedow entered the medical department of the same institution, and received his diploma therefrom in 1902.

After his graduation Dr. Wiedow completed his studies with a six months course in Vienna and Berlin, taking a special course in bloodless surgery, as advocated by Dr. Adolph Lorenz, of international fame. Returning from his European studies, Dr. Wiedow began the practice of his profession at Round Lake, where he was located two years. On January 1, 1904, he came to Worthington, opened an office, and has since been engaged in the practice of his chosen profession. Dr. Wiedow was married at Victor, Iowa, July 4, 1900, to Miss Cora Simpson, daughter of Mr. and Mrs. G.G. Simpson. Both the doctor and his wife are members of the Presbyterian church.

On July 1, 1908, Dr. B.O. Mork of Yellow Medicine, Minnesota, a graduate of the Hamline University and Hamline Medical School, formed a partnership with Dr. Henry Wiedow, the firm being now styled Wiedow & Mork."

# Appendix C

# OBITUARY, DR. HENRY WIEDOW

In the 20 December 1940 edition of the newspaper, The Desert Trail, Twentynine Palms, California we find:

**"Dr. Wiedow, Local Physician and Surgeon Suddenly Taken by Death; Believed to Have Suffered Heart Attack While Driving Car**

Funeral of Dr. Henry Wiedow was held this (Friday) forenoon in the Little Church of the Desert at Twentynine Palms, with Dr. C.C. Williamson, the minister, conducting the service. Fatal accident befell Dr. Wiedow last Tuesday evening about 5:30 o'clock when, supposedly stricken with a heart attack, he was found dead under his overturned coupe on the Two-Mile road a short distance east of the post office.

When he left his hospital a few minutes previous to the fatality, he remarked to his daughter Edythe that he was very tired, and as yet he had three calls to make before he would return for the evening.

Friends gathering to pay their last respects filled the church. Dr. James W. Martin of Pasadena, long-time friend of the family, sang "The Old Rugged Cross," "In the Garden" and "Crossing the Bar," to the accompaniment of Ruth Nichoes at the piano.

The body will rest beside that of Mrs. Wiedow in the Grand View Mausoleum, Glendale. Dr. Robert L. Evans, retired minister of the Lincoln Avenue Presbyterian Church in Pasadena, will officiate at the committal at Grand View. Dr. Wiedow was an elder of the Lincoln Avenue Presbyterian Church. Brother Kiwanians will have charge at the last rites.

Dr. Wiedow was called at the age of 67. Born in Clayton County, Iowa in 1873, he finished his preparatory schooling and then was graduated from the University of Iowa medical branch, completing that work in 1902. He then spent two years at the University of Berlin, in Germany, where he took a post-graduate course in surgery. In Berlin it was he studied under two of the world's finest surgeons at the time, Adolph Lorenz and von Bergman, one of whom was the originator of bloodless surgery. Surgeon von Bergman was the personal physician of Kaiser Wilhelm.

For 20 years Dr. Wiedow practiced medicine and surgery at Worthington, Minnesota, and it was during the World War he served as head of the Minnesota State Medical Advisory Board. For this service he was cited by President Wilson who presented him with a medal.

Further study in surgery by Dr. Wiedow was at the Mayo Clinic, Rochester, Minnesota.

It was during his last year of study at the University of Iowa he was married, Mrs. Wiedow preceding him in death in 1928.

Coming to Altadena from Worthington in 1923, he practiced until 1936 when his health failed and he came to Twentynine Palms, seeking the climate as a relief. Almost immediately he rallied and it was then his idea of a hospital for Twentynine Palms was born. The present 29 Palms hospital is a monument to Dr. Wiedow. Alone he built most of the first rock-laid unit which for several years served as a combined home, office and surgery. Gradually expansion took place until now a dozen or more convalescents can be cared for.

Dr. Wiedow contributed largely to all civic and community affairs, was benevolent in the founding of our local church, was a member of the local Lions Club, and a life member of the Altadena Kiwanis Club as well as a member of the American Medical Association. He also held the government appointment to care for World War veterans locally.

Surviving him are two sisters, Mrs. Bertha Nyweide of Muscatine, Iowa and Mrs. Mary Sheppard of Owossa, Michigan, a brother, Charles Wiedow of victor, Iowa, and his daughter, Mrs. William Phelps, who will carry on the institution and convalescent home as founded by her father.

Pallbearers were brother Lions, Walt Berg, Frank Bagley, Ted Holderman and Bill Underhill; William Hazlett of Los Angeles, a life-long friend, and Henry Oleson. Reynolds & Eberle, Pasadena morticians, were in charge of the funeral.

The Desert Trail joins friends of the family in heartfelt sympathies to the bereaved."

One week later, in the same newspaper, we find in the editorial section:

### "Henry Wiedow – Physician

Probably no happening in Twentynine Palms has ever caused such widespread sorrow as the sudden passing of Henry Wiedow, physician. It was at the dawn of evening when this warrior in the army of the faithful heard the command of the great Captain to halt. It all happened at the end of a perfect day for Henry Wiedow ... perfect because he was privileged to minister to suffering humanity up to the very moment of his departure. In an instant he was at work in 'another room.'

This is just as he had wished it to be – no pause between his work here and his work there. 'Just three more calls and I will come home and rest,' were his parting words as he left to keep his rendezvous with death. He kept that rendezvous and went home.

A consistent Christian, an exceptionally capable physician, a kindly man. His deeds are immortal."

# Appendix D

# LETTERS FROM EDIE WIEDOW

Particularly for the insights to Dr. Henry Wiedow which they might provide, two letters from his adopted daughter, Edythe Ann (Edie), are provided here. The first letter was written twelve days after Henry passed away and was addressed to Edie's Aunt Bertha (Wiedow) Nyweide. The Charlie whom she mentions in the Postscript must be her Uncle Charlie Wiedow. The letter was made available by Bertha's grandson, Bill Nyweide. The second letter was written when Edie was 71 years of age, i.e., almost 50 years later, and was addressed to Sharon McKay, daughter of Edie's cousin, Alice (Wiedow) Wolf. It was in response to Sharon's expressed interest in information for her family-history project – and is therefore wonderfully enlightening. It was made available by Sharon McKay.

**P.O. Box 61**                                    **Telephone 302**
**TWENTYNINE PALMS EMERGENCY HOSPITAL AND SANITARIUM**

**Henry Wiedow, M.D., Medical Director**
**Twentynine Palms, California**
April December 29, 1940

Dearest Aunt Bertha,

Thank you very much for your lovely letter and your offer to come. I know you cannot afford the trip and I am not alone. I was married the 7th of September, 1939 just after I returned from my last visit to you.

I sent you a gift which Daddy had purchased for you just a short time before he was taken. I thought you would appreciate it doubly as you see he was thinking of you up to the last minute. I think you know how much he loved you Aunt Bertha. You were always so kind about remembering him on every little occasion and although he was too busy or too tired to write to you often, it didn't mean that he didn't often think of you.

Daddy had been up and going to the last minute. He had been failing I think the last month though he never said anything to me because he was too kind to want me to be upset or worried over him. I can see now that he looked a little tired and a little more short of breath but at the time I felt that he would be alright in a few days as he usually was with a little rest. I was down in bed with the flu which he was so afraid would turn into pneumonia when he was taken from me. It is pretty lonesome even though I try not to miss him too much because I know he is so much better off. It was just such a shock that I still cannot believe it. He went as he always wanted to go, while out making his calls and while ministering to other people. He had just worked too hard.

I am sending you a paper with an editorial that was written for my daddy and which shows very plainly how everyone in this community worshiped him. I'm so proud that I was his daughter and that I was the one to have the chance to make him happy, for he deserved the best it was possible to give a human being.

Thank you for wanting to come, perhaps Bill and I can pay you a visit this summer. We want to. Write me please.

Love

Bill and Edie Phelps

P.S. Excuse the mistakes – I haven't heard a word from Charlie – Do you suppose he didn't receive my letter?

June 9, 1990

Dear Sharon,

I can't begin to tell you how interested I was to receive your letter this morning. Strange as it is going to sound, for the past few weeks I have been having the name "Wiedow" break into my thoughts out of nowhere! It was getting a little spooky since I imagined that I was about the end of the line of my generation and it made me wonder if by any chance any of the cousins that I know as a child were still alive. Those I remember the best were Uncle Charlie and Aunt Velma's kids since every two years until the time of my mother's passing away in 1928, we visited the farm and what wonderful memories I have of those times. Being an only child, sleeping in a room with the cousins was just wonderful. I even remember a big pine tree just outside the window of the bedroom that I could see at night. Harold was the oldest and much too sophisticated to bother with the rest of us. I think it was Leon

(?) who occasionally teased us, but it was Violet and Alice whom I dearly loved. Alice I see is your mother, correct? She used to receive some of my hand-me-downs and I remember causing a rumpus because I had a blue and white sun dress that I was glued into, that my mom gave to her and I didn't want anyone else to have it. I always was a clothes horse even as a tiny one!!

I remember walking along the dirt road and picking some kind of berries, currents I think, wrapping them in a clean white cloth with sugar and then sucking the juice! Right now I can't remember the day or date or sometimes even my own name!!!! Strange, isn't it, how a letter can bring back to many memories. I also remember the chiggers in the grass. Everyone sat outside at night and they would bite my feet and ankles until I could hardly walk on my swollen feet. We also caught fireflies in a bottle. That was wonderful, for in California we didn't have such things, chiggers either, thank goodness.

A few years ago, we were camping in Iowa in our trailer not far from Fort Dodge and my husband, a native Californian, called me to come out and see the sparks landing in the grass from someone's campfire. When I explained that they were bugs with lights in their tails, he looked at me as though I had lost my mind. Our son discovered them a few years ago for the first time and couldn't believe them either.

One of the things I remember about Harold was that, when he graduated from High School, my Dad had promised to give him his gold pocket watch. I wonder if he still has it or if, like most things, it has gone the way of so many broken, useless objects that we have no real interest in when we are young.

Like you, I often think with fond memories of the stories and questions that I could have asked while there was still someone left to answer them for me. I'm thrilled that you have found such in interesting hobby. It is amazing how many people I have met who are really into genealogy these days.

As you may or may not know, I was adopted by Cora and Henry, having been born in the Worthington, Minn. hospital which was owned by them. My mother died shortly after my birth and I never left the Wiedow home. I was officially adopted by them at about six months of age. I was given the opportunity to know about my mother, father, brother and the many relatives on both sides of the family, so I think that tells you what sort of a caring person my father was. I still have an aunt on my natural mother's

154

side and my older brother who are still living and with whom I keep in contact, but no blood relative ever took the place of the Wiedow's in my heart. My husband and I adopted a son at birth in 1950 and we gave him the name of William Wiedow Welch as my way of perpetuating my name. He is now 40 years old and would have been a joy to his grandfather.

I never knew the names of Grandma and Grandpa Wiedow. Grandpa must have died before my birth and Grossmutter, as we called her, lived with Aunt Bertha until her death. She always seemed to love me when she visited us in California or when we went to see her at Aunt Bertha's. She spoke very broken English and Bertha talked to her almost entirely in German. My Dad could not speak much German and, being the oldest, I have wondered if Grandpa Wiedow was born in this country or perhaps lived here for a long time for none of the family that I can remember had the least bit of an accent. I have never yet met a German person who seemed to know the spelling as Wiedow. I have seen it spelled other ways. Do you know anything about that? Was it changed or Americanized in some way?

I have a picture of Dad that is very good which I shall try to get a copy made from the machine at the library. Also anything else I may have that would give you some interesting information about him.

To respond to your inquiry about his habits, etc.: He attended and participated in church services, was a charter member of the Pasadena Lion's Club, worked with underprivileged children, dresses as Santa Claus for the neighborhood children on Christmas Eve, and had a warm caring personality which gave him a wonderful rapport with his patients. Incidently, in case you would like to know, he graduated from the University of Minnesota Medical School, class of 1902. *(Note by author: Henry graduated from the University of Iowa in 1902, documented by a transcript from the College. See Fig. 11.1.)* He and my mother made trips to Germany in 1911 and 1913 so that he could study the latest surgery methods under what were then considered the finest surgeons in the world. One of the reasons that I know that his German was very limited was because of the stories he used to tell of trying to explain to a policeman that he was lost and needed directions. He had a great sense of humor. He owned the Worthington city Hospital, the only one in town. Sold it when he became too ill to practice regularly anymore, which must have been about 1921 or

155

1922. He had tuberculosis and made several trips to California for his health, and that is how he moved to Altadena (California) where we continued to live until he again moved for his health to 29 Palms, California in 1937, where the dry desert air gave him a few more years to live. He died in 1940, just short of his 68th birthday which he would have celebrated on January 5, 1941.

I do not know the whereabouts of any of my mother's family. She was born Cora Simpson. I do remember Grandpa Simpson and remember visiting him in Aberdeen, South Dakota, but he must have passed away before my mother did. She died in February 1928. She was born in 1869 and was four years older than my father. She was a school teacher and I am sure helped him get started in his practice. He worked his way through college and medical school, and I remember him saying that, after he had worked long hours, he would have to come back to his room and then study late into the night. He couldn't afford a haircut and so would hold his hair back out of his eyes while he studied with a couple of small combs. One morning, he left for class with the combs still in his hair and so acquired the name of "side-combs" from his classmates.

I guess I should have mentioned that the last time I saw Uncle Charlie and Aunt Velda was in 1938 when I drove through Victor in order to see them. They were living in town, I believe, at the time and they were so gracious and glad to visit with me and a friend who was accompanying me to New York to see the World's Fair as a graduation present for me. I also spent a couple of days and nights with Margaret Willard and her family in Ann Arbor and had a wonderful time. Her daughter Ann was attending the University, I believe, and she had a lovely dinner party for us attended by some of her friends. I must have been 19 then. Margaret Sheppard kept in touch by a Christmas letter until her death a few years ago. I have pictures of Margaret, Harriet and one of her other sisters at our home in Altadena when I would guess that I was approximately 6 years old, as my mother was in the pictures too. I can't remember Margaret Sheppard's mother's name for some reason, except that I know she had 3 or 4 daughters and was married to a Chiropractor or an Osteopath and they sent all the girls to Ann Arbor where they all received their Master's Degrees. A truly intelligent family and they loved life to the fullest.

I forgot about Dad's physical appearance. He was about 5'11" when he was younger but, like most folks, seemed to be shorter before his death, perhaps because of his illness. He weighed about 165 lbs., had light brown hair and very blue eyes, and I considered him a very handsome man.

I remember vaguely having heard from someone that he and my mother had a son who died in infancy. This may or may not be correct. I don't know if this child was born in Worthington or not. It would have been long before my birth. I do hope that I have been able to give you at least a little of the information that you are looking for. I would like to have your mother see this and perhaps she will remember what fun we had together as children. I would be interested to know how many of Uncle Charlie's children are still living, and also if Bertha's son is still alive.

This has really been such fun and perhaps someday we will hear from you again. That is, if you have made it this far!!

Since I am not a real branch of the family tree, I will not fill out the page about us, but you might like to know that I am 71 years old, in good health, a mother and wife. I have never really worked except to care for my home. I am a real nest builder. Love to cook, decorate, do both oil and water color paintings, lots of knitting, and crochet some afghans to keep my hands busy while the TV is going. I also china paint.

My husband Bill and I were married in Feb. of 1946 when he returned from the war. He is now 73, very handsome, loves to play bridge and mess around in his vegetable garden, which seems to thrive in spite of all the things he does to it! He was a plumber in Pasadena until his retirement in 1976, when we moved here to Minden. He also is a retired Lt. Col. in the USAF and we go to Sacramento once a month to pick up our prescriptions and do some shopping at the Commissary and the Base Exchange. It is about 100 miles from here over the mountain and a beautiful ride. We just make a day of it. We have a son, Bill, born in 1950, as I told you. He has always had a deep love for the outdoors. Probably because we have had a trailer since he was 3 years old and have done lots of traveling with him. Last year he hiked the Appalachian Trail, 2100 miles, from Atlanta, Georgia at its beginning, all the way to the end at Mt. Katadin, Maine. It took him 5-1/2 months and he had quite an experience. He has also hiked the Pacific Crest Trail from Mexico to Canada and this summer he will do a part of the new central trail through the Rockies starting at Yellowstone and going to the Tetons. About a 6-week hike. Needless to say, he is not married and has no obligations. When Bill retired, I drew up

157

the plans for our home and we, the three of us, built this home. It took us a whole year but it is truly home and we love it. We live at the foot of the Sierra's on the high desert, just a few miles from Carson City, Nevada, and about the same distance from Lake Tahoe. Unless I think of something else, I'll try to get this off in tomorrow morning's mail and will be glad to hear from you again.

With love,<br>
Edie

# Appendix E

# LETTERS FROM HAMBURG

These two letters were written to Maria Sophia Catharina <u>Dorothea</u> (nee Schlichting) Jahlas. She was the widow of <u>Johann</u> Jochim Jahlas, who was one of the two men killed in the train accident of 27 July 1895. (See Chapter 8.) Johann and Dorothea were both born in Glaisin, he 7 Dec. 1850 and she 13 Sept. 1854. Both immigrated in 1895. The writer of the letters was the widow of Jochim August Heinrich Ludwig Schlichting, brother of <u>Dorothea</u> (Schlichting) Jahlas. He was born 29 Oct. 1851 in Glaisin and died in 1915 in Hamburg. Mr. Fruend, to whom the first letter was addressed, was perhaps Johann Heinrich F.L. Fruendt, born 10 July 1851, immigrated in 1880. The letters express not only empathy for Dorothea Jahlas' loss but also (even more strongly) the writer's feelings of despair which followed WWI. Copies of these letters were provided the present author by descendants of the Jahlas family, namely by Bill and Ruth Jahlas of Deep River, Iowa.

Hamburg
5 July 1925

Dear Mr. Fruend,
   Please forgive me for burdening you with a letter. The sender of this letter is Mrs. Jahlas' sister-in-law. I learned of your address from Jochim Fehlov; his sister-in-law visited him 14 days ago in Glaisin. Now would you do me the favor of letting my sister-in-law know and ask her to write me sometime. Also you. Hopefully all is well with her children.
   I have to share with you, dear Sister-in-law, that I had many losses during the war. Dear Sister-in-Law, already in 1915 my husband died of a heart attack. He had worried too much about his children. I had 4 sons in the war and 3 of them were killed. Dear Sister-in-Law, I would have written to you already during the war if I had had your address. Dear Sister-in-Law, I have been alone now already 10 years. I have rented a room – I have to pay 10

Marks. I get from social security 6 Marks per week. One can't do much with that, and I can't work any more. I am now 76. I can't live with my children – they don't have enough room. So I have no choice but to live alone. Now, dear Sister-in-Law, I hope that, since I write to you, you don't take me for a good-for-nothing.

Mr. Fründ also visited us once in Hamburg when my husband was still alive. I can't believe that my husband didn't take down your address. He spoke of it then.

Dear Sister-in-Law, when you went to America, you also lost your husband soon. It was terrible when we heard that. I still have the letter from him in which he wrote that he wanted above all to go to America. That was 27 March 1895. Ya, that is already a long time ago. Now dear Sister-in-Law, be so good as to write to me also once. I would be very pleased if you would do me that favor. Dear Sister-in-Law, I give you my address:

Frau Schlichting
Henderstrasse 11, Apt. 5
Barmbeck
Hamburg 21

Hamburg
3 January

Dear Sister-in-Law and all your children,

The best New Year's wishes. Did you make a good start into the new year? The main thing is if one is healthy. And then, dear Sister-in-Law, my hearty thanks for your dear letter with its contents and the nice photos. I was so pleased. And then you asked if I also prayed for your brother; how I sat beside him by the bed and prayed. The dear God, he does burden me though; all of my children were in the war and I was entirely alone. But the dear God wanted it otherwise. He was always understanding. He always took care of our children when he passed away. Then for the burial all of the children came home from the war. Including all sons-in-law. I followed him. The burial was nice. But, dear Sister-in-Law, it was too sad – I didn't have a Pfennig. I went at the end of the funeral procession. And then they told me that he should pay another 3 Marks, and he didn't have that – and didn't get any money. And none of the children had any since they were all in the war. Then I arranged for installment payments

160

– the entire funeral. I also arranged for installment payments on a separate lot. Also a nice stone and a saying carved in the stone. The saying reads: <u>His going to sleep and passing on begins the rest of his life.</u> Then I had to make payments for a long time, and you know, dear Sister-in-Law, that we had so little to eat. Was it so also for you, or did you always have something to eat? Here we had to make our way through.

And then you asked how many children I have. I had eight. Three were killed in the war. Now I have still three girls; one son, who is 35, is not yet married.

Now, dear Sister-in-Law, I want you to know that I still go regularly to church and pray for all of you. Today is New Years Day. I go every week. That is all there is for me. I have nothing else since my children have for themselves nothing. I enclose 2 pictures. We get those in the church. On Saturdays we get good cake and coffee and a book for singing. That is a nice hour.

Dear Sister-in-Law, once again many thanks and write again soon. Many greetings to you and your children.

# Appendix F

# OTHER WIEDOW FAMILIES

Carl Wiedow's family emigrated from Glaisin; Carl was born in Bellevue (today Margarethenhof), his father in Sülze, and his grandfather in Kleeste (Brandenburg). During my researches on this family, I became involved in researches on three other Wiedow families – motivated sometimes by my desire to identify those Wiedows related to Carl and sometimes in order to help family members with their family histories. More specifically, I became involved with researches on a family with roots in Leussow and Bresegard which also settled in Clayton County, Iowa; a second family with roots in Liepe, Grittel and Boek which settled near Fairmont, Minnesota; and a third family which still lives in Bresegard. The family from Leussow came to my attention at the same time that I found the Carl Wiedow records – they lived in the same township in Clayton County as Carl Wiedow and went to the same church. Hence researches were necessary in order to sort out the two families. The Leussow family immigrated relatively early – in 1851, i.e., already 17 years earlier than Carl Wiedow. I have found no hint (marriage records, baptism records, etc.) of contact between these two families. The husband, Johann, served as a volunteer from October 1862 until May 1864 in the 6th Iowa Cavalry. This cavalry waged in 1863 (Battle of White Stone Hills) and 1864 (Upper Missouri Expedition) the last two attacks against the Indians in Iowa. In contrast to Carl Wiedow, Johann was unable to write – his signature was an X. His wife, Sophia Heidtmann, was unusually fertile and strong. I have found records for 17 children; according to the 1900 US census, she gave birth to 19 children; the church records imply that her last child was Number 21. She nevertheless reached the age of 81! Two descendants who became aware of my researches on Wiedow families have inquired about their backgrounds.

In March 1998, shortly after I published my first article on the Carl Wiedow family, Carol Madsen, a descendant of a Wiedow family which had settled near Fairmont, Minnesota, contacted me – wondering if her family might be related to Carl Wiedow. Fortunately, she had relatively detailed information about her immigrant ancestors, i.e., relatively precise names and birth dates of her grandmother and four siblings, her great grandfather and two brothers, and her greatgrandmother. She knew that her greatgrandmother was born in Bockup, but had no clue from which village the Wiedow family came. But the information sufficed to establish quickly that this family came from Liepe, and that the records showed no connection with the Carl Wiedow family. In spite of other commitments, I was able to send her two weeks later a family tree going back to 1780 – the year of the church fire in Eldena. In July 1998 I met Fritz Witt, living now in Radolfzell but born in Liepe, and mentioned to him Carol Madsen and her Wiedow connection. Carol was unbelievably lucky! Witt is not only born in Liepe but is also author of the booklet, "Dorfgeschichten aus Liepe." (Village stories from Liepe) I translated for Carol those paragraphs which dealt with her family. A comparison of Carol's family tree with that for Witt revealed that they had common ancestors–the most recent being Carol's Greatgreatgreatgrandparents, Jochim Christian Wiedow and his wife Christina Elisabeth Jastram, married in 1808 in Dömitz. In the fall of 1998, Witt visited descendants of this Wiedow family in Liepe and told them about the relatives in America. The family brought out three photos from America from about 1885. They knew that these photos came from one of the Wiedows who had emigrated, but had no idea who the people in the photos were. From copies sent to Carol, she was able to identify the house and the people in the photos. In 2002, Rolf Gödecke from Hamburg, Fritz Witt and I (all with significant ties to Mecklenburg) conducted a two-day Genealogy Symposium in Liepe. Carol Madsen was the guest of honor.

The Wiedow family in Bresegard entered the picture initially because I anticipated that Carl Wiedow's family stemmed from Bresegard. My initial motivation was extinguished when I determined that Carl Wiedow's family was not related to this family, but it was rekindled by the interest expressed by Karin Wiedow from Bresegard. From another source, and according to oral family tradition, a Heinrich Wiedow from Bresegard emigrated to America late in the 19th century, founded a successful tobacco business and died with no heirs in the USA. But the family in Bresegard was not able to obtain sufficient details to collect inheritance.

Ahnentafels (family trees) for these three Wiedow families are included here. In each case, in order to respect the privacy of the families even though more recent data is on hand, the starting point for the Ahnentafel is chosen for a birth at least 100 years ago. No common Wiedow ancestor has been found for these several families. The assistance of Gödecke and Witt with the Ahnentafels for the families from Liepe and Bresegard is appreciated greatly.

## 1st GENERATION

1 Charles Wiedow: b 1903

## 2nd GENERATION

2 Johan Karl Wiedow: b 23 Dec 1862  Garnavillo,Iowa; m Abt 1899
3 Agnes Krosling: b Abt 1879  Germany

## 3rd GENERATION

4 Johann Juergen Friedrich Christian Wiedow [Farmer]: b 23 Nov 1824  Leussow; m Aug 1851  Garnavillo,Iowa; d 21
  Apr 1896  Garnavillo,Iowa
5 Friedrica Elisabeth Dorothea Catharina Heidtmann: b  7 Apr 1826  Leussow; d 21 Oct 1907  Garnavillo,Iowa

## 4th GENERATION

8 Johann Juergen Christian Wiedow [Knecht]: b 13 Jan 1800  Leussow; d 16 Nov 185?
9 Trien Maria Friederica Baetke: b 14 Dec 1800  Leussow; d 1876
10 Johann Friedrich Heidtmann [Rademacher]: b 29 Apr 1792  Redefin; m 26 Jun 1821  Leussow
11 Carolina Maria Charlotta Otten: b  9 Oct 1804  Leussow

## 5th GENERATION

16 Johann Peter Wiedow [Hauswirth]: b 21 Mar 1761  Bresegard; m  5 Dec 1794  Leussow; d 17 Nov 1829  Leussow
17 Ann Liese Saumann: b 11 Jun 1759  Goehlen
18 Cord Jochen Baetke [Einwohner]: b  7 Mar 1766  Leussow; m 14 Jan 1800  Leussow
19 Trien Liese Schmidt: b  5 May 1769  Leussow
20 Juergen Ernst Heidtmann [Einvohner]: b Redefin; m 22 Jan 1790  Alt Jabel
21 Dorothea Elisabeth Jewe: b Luebbendorf?
22 Diederich Otten [Rademacher]: b Abt 1775  ; d 16 Mar 1819  Leussow
23 Anna Maria Schoen: b 22 Nov 1780  Neuhof

## 6th GENERATION

32 Hans Juergen Wiedow [Hauswirth]: b Abt 1723  ; d 21 May 1790  Bresegard
33 Anna Ilsabe Geister: b Abt 1727  ; d 19 Oct 1797  Bresegard
34 Claas Juergen Saumann [Hauswirth]: b 22 Feb 1719  Goehlen?; m  9 Nov 1745  Leussow; d 17 May 1776  Goehlen
35 Trien Liese Schroeder: b 16 Jun 1728  Goehlen; d 28 Jan 1808  Goehlen
36 Hans Jochen Cord Baetke [Knecht]: b Lenzwisch,Brandenburg; m 16 Nov 1764  Leussow
37 Ann Liese Schlubeck: b Leussow?
38 Johann Friderich Schmidt [Huthmann]: b 15 May 1744  Loosen; m 22 Feb 1765  Leussow
39 Julian Lies Thees: b 14 Feb 1748  Goehlen
40 Hans Jochim Heidtmann: m 29 Apr 1757  ; Alt Jabel
41 Cathrin Sophie Martens
42 Jochim Christian Jewe [Hauswirth]

## 7th GENERATION

68 Jochim Saumann [Hauswirth]: c 24 Jan 1679  Leussow; m 18 Nov 1710  Leussow
69 Catrin Dorothia Luethe: c  1 Jan 1689  Leussow
70 Christian Schroeder [Hauswirth]: c 18 Sep 1680  Leussow; m  1 Dec 1715  Leussow; d Bef 1746  Goehlen
71 Catrin Dorothea von Sinnen: c  3 Feb 1692  Leussow; d  3 Nov 1743  Goehlen
72 Christian Baetke [Einwohner]
74 Jakob Schlubeck [Zimmermann]: d Bef 1765
76 Peter Schmidt [Hauswirth]: c 14 Apr 1705  Leussow; m 20 May 1732  Leussow

165

77 Ann Ilse Busche: c 22 Jan 1712  Leussow
78 Erdmann Friedrich Thees [Hauswirth]: c 13 Oct 1683  Leussow; m  4 Dec 1744  Leussow
79 Dorothea Palms: c  1 Sep 1711  Leussow

## 8th GENERATION

136 Hans Saumann: m  2 Nov 1674  ; Leussow
137 Catrin Palms
138 Hans Luethe
139 Catrin Mincke
140 Christian Schroeder: b Goehlen?; m 28 Oct 1678  Leussow
141 Anna Benuer
142 Hans von Sinnen [Hauswirth]: m 12 Jul 1676  ; Leussow
143 Ilse Saumann
152 Peter Schmidt [Hauswirth]: m 18 Nov 1691  ; Leussow
153 Sophia Losen
154 Jochim Busche [Hauswirth]: m  8 Nov 1707  ; Leussow
155 Cathrin Sasch
156 Hans Thees
157 Catrin Rodker (?)
158 Hinrich Palms [Schneider]: m 22 Nov 1700  ; Leussow
159 Catrin Warncken

166

1st GENERATION

1 Martha Wilhelmina Minna Wiedow: b 30 Sep 1882  Bockup; m 23 Sep 1902  ; d 14 May 1943  Lake Belt Township,
  Martin County,Minnesota

2nd GENERATION

2 Friederich Jochim Juergen Wiedow [Farmer]: b  8 Jul 1852  Liepe; d  1 Sep 1889  Ceylon,Minnesota
3 Maria Dorothea Katharina Stolte: b 25 Sep 1852  Bockup; d 22 Mar 1935  Lake Belt Twp,Minnesota

3rd GENERATION

4 Johann Jochim Wiedow [Buedner]: b 12 May 1809  Grittel; m  8 Apr 1842  Eldena; d 12 Apr 1889  Liepe
5 Marie Dorothee Boettcher: b 21 Feb 1813  Boeck; d  5 Apr 1883
6 Johann Joachim Juergen Franz Stolte [Buedner]: b  7 Mar 1821  Bockup; m 21 Nov 1851  Bockup; d  8 Aug 1878
7 Anna Carolina Katharina Sophia Lucia Eva Schult: b 10 Feb 1823  Polz

4th GENERATION

8 Jochim Christian Wiedow [Hauswirth]: b  3 Nov 1763  Boek; m 29 Jan 1808  Eldena; d 21 Apr 1839  Grittel
9 Christina Elisabeth Jastram: b 29 Sep 1780  Polz; d  4 Jan 1818  Grittel
10 Johan Jacob Boettcher [Hauswirth]: b  9 Mar 1773  Boeck; m 19 Jun 1792  Gorlosen; d 15 Feb 1838  Boek
11 Marie Dorthie Benoer: b  4 Mar 1772  Goehlen; d 31 Jan 1841  Boek
12 Jacob Heinrich Stolte [Einwohner]: b  5 Oct 1788  Suelze; m  6 Dec 1816  Bockup
13 Anna Elisabeth Becker: b 26 Oct 1790  Strassen
14 Juergen Heinrich Schult [Hauswirth]: b 30 Nov 1780  Polz; m 17 Apr 1812  Doemitz
15 Elisabeth Dorothea Wiedow: b 24 Aug 1792  Grittel

5th GENERATION

16 Johann Jochim Jacob Wiedow [Schulze]: b 1720  Boek
17 Catharina Maria Franck: b Abt 1726  ; d  2 Nov 1784  Boek
18 Johann Hartwig Jastram [Hausmann]: b Strassen?; m  7 Nov 1769  Doemitz
19 Liese Dorthie Rieve: c 13 Sep 1747  Doemitz
20 J. Niklas Boettcher [Hauswirth]: b Abt 1729  ; d 25 Jan 1799  Boek
21 M. Brencken: b Abt 1733  ; d  9 Oct 1793  Boek
22 Jochim Christian Benoer [Hauswirth]: c 16 Feb 1723  Leussow; m 15 Feb 1771  Leussow
23 Marie Greth Schroeder: b Abt 1732  ; d 22 May 1776  Goehlen
24 Friedrich Stolte [Arbeitsmann]
25 Dorothea Kaakstein
26 Jochen Christian Becker [Einwohner]: c  7 Aug 1752  Conow; m 11 Nov 1788  Eldena
27 Maria Elisabeth Meyer
28 Hinnerich Peter Schult [Hausmann]: c 30 Apr 1738  Doemitz; m 26 Nov 1767  Doemitz; d 10 Nov 1799  Polz
29 Trien Ilsche Fehrmann: c 30 Apr 1738  Doemitz; d 14 Nov 1811  Polz
30 Jochim Christian Wiedow [Hauswirth]: b  3 Nov 1763  Boek; m 23 Jul 1789  Eldena; d 21 Apr 1839  Grittel
31 Anna Catharina Jastram: b Abt 1757  ; d 27 Oct 1807  Grittel

6th GENERATION

36 Jochim Jastram [Hausmann]: b Abt 1710  ; bu 25 May 1784  Eldena
37 Marckwardt: bu 25 May 1784  ; Eldena
38 Hans Juergen Rieve [Hausmann]: c 27 Dec 1717  Doemitz; m 27 Oct 1746  Doemitz
39 Agneta Jastram: b Abt 1720  Grittel?
44 Hans Benoer [Hauswirth]: b Goehlen?; m 25 Nov 1721  Leussow
45 Catharina Duede
52 Martin Becker [Hauswirth]: m  2 Dec 1749  ; Conow

53 Anna Margaretha Karmaus: b Dec 1708  Niendorf
54 Jochim Jacob Meyer [Buedner]: b Abt 1734  ; d  4 Jan 1813  Strassen
56 Jacob Schult: m 18 Nov 1717  ; Doemitz; d Bef 1756
57 Trien Lise Francke
58 Hans Hinrich Fehrmann [Vieter]: c  5 Sep 1697  Doemitz; m 10 Jul 1737  Doemitz
59 Catharina Ilsabe Stoeter
60 Johann Jochim Wiedow [Schulze]
61 Catharina Maria Franck: b Abt 1726  ; d  2 Nov 1784  Boek
62 Peter Jacob Jastram [Hauswirth]

## 7th GENERATION

 76 Jochim Rieve [Hausmann]: b Mar 1676  Polz; m 22 Nov 1713  Doemitz
 77 Catharina Albers
 78 Jochim Jastram [Hausmann]: b Grittel?; bu 21 May 1782  Eldena
 88 Jochim Benoer: m 30 Oct 1676  ; Leussow
 89 Maria Kofahls
104 Martin Becker [Hauswirth]
106 Jochim Karmaus [Hauswirth]: b Niendorf?; m 17 Oct 1699  Conow
107 Trin Lies Schult
116 Otto Johan Fehrmann [Schuster]: m 25 Sep 1696  ; Doemitz; d 18 Jan 1739
117 Anna Albrechts: d  7 Dec 1738
118 Hinrich Stoeter [Hausmann]

## 8th GENERATION

152 Jochim Rieve [Einlieger]: m 14 Oct 1673  ; Doemitz
153 Catharina Albers
212 Peter Karmaus
214 Peter Schult

## 9th GENERATION

304 Asmus Rieve
306 Hans Albers [Ackersmann]
307 Catharina Baljken

168

## 1st GENERATION

1 Otto Johannes Wilhelm Karl Wiedow: b 26 Jul 1909  Bresegard; d 16 Oct 1985  Bresegard

## 2nd GENERATION

2 Heinrich Friedrich Erdman Wiedow: b 20 Apr 1879  Bresegard; m 29 Nov 1907  Bresegard; d 22 Mar 1954
   Bresegard
3 Martha Frieda Elisabeth Marie Westphal: b 10 Feb 1886  Bresegard; d 15 Jan 1973  Bresegard

## 3rd GENERATION

4 Johann Christian Friederich Wiedow [Hauswirth]: b 21 May 1838  Bresegard; m  2 Sep 1873  Eldena; d  8 Jul
   1900  Bresegard
5 Dorothea Marie Wilhelmine Hinrichs: b 12 Jan 1851  Conow; d  2 Oct 1932  Bresegard
6 Carl August Wilhelm Westphal: b 23 Dec 1852  Neu Karstaedt; m 13 Feb 1880  Eldena
7 Dorothea Carolina Wilhelmine Stiel: b 14 Apr 1863  Bresegard

## 4th GENERATION

8 Jochim Christian Wiedow: b 28 Dec 1811  Bresegard; m 20 Jun 1837  Eldena; d 22 Oct 1876  Bresegard
9 Charlotte Catharina Elisabeth Bruening: b 22 Jan 1812  Croon
10 Johann Jochim Erdman Hinrichs: b 28 Sep 1815  Conow; m  1 Dec 1840  Conow; d  5 Mar 1884  Conow
11 Katharina Elisabeth Dorothea Timmermann: b 10 Dec 1815  Alt Krenzlin; d  8 Jun 1888
12 Johann Joachim Christian Friedrich Westphal [Buedner]: b  4 Aug 1820  Karstaedt
13 Anna Catharina Sophia Dorothea Gaeth: b Leussow
14 Johann Jochim Jacob Stiel: b 21 May 1833  Bresegard; m  2 Feb 1860  Eldena; d 24 Aug 1865  Bresegard
15 Maria Dorothea Johanna Schroeder: b 24 Sep 1837  Glaisin

## 5th GENERATION

16 Jochim Christoph Wiedow: c  1 Nov 1782  Eldena; m  3 Dec 1805  Eldena; d 15 Nov 1813  Bresegardt
17 Catharina Dorothea Dien: b 24 Apr 1786  Bresegardt
18 Johann Friederich Bruening [Hauswirth]: b 14 Aug 1783  Krohn; m 29 May 1809  Eldena
19 Catharina Margaretha Elisabeth Luetcke: b 27 Aug 1779  Niendorf; d 30 Mar 1839  Krohn
20 Jochim Erdman Hinrichs [Hauswirth]: b  2 Aug 1780  Grebs; m 24 Jan 1804  Conow; d 12 Apr 1834  Conow
21 Catharina Elisabeth Sass: b  1 Jan 1779  Conow; d 11 Aug 1839
24 Carl August Westphal
25 Sophia Dreier
28 Johann Heinrich Stiel [Hauswirth]: b  8 Nov 1800  Bresegard; m 23 Jul 1830  Eldena; d 24 Oct 1841  Bresegar
29 Elisabeth Maria Hann: b 10 Oct 1812  Malk
30 Johann Juergen Daniel Schroeder [Einwohner]: b 30 Jan 1806  Glaisin; m  1 Mar 1836  Eldena
31 Maria Elisabeth Schneider: b  1 Jan 1808  Glaisin

## 6th GENERATION

32 Jochim Wiedow [Hauswirth]: b 1747  Bresegardt; d 28 Oct 1828  Bresegardt
33 Anna Catharina Jungbluth: c 10 Jul 1758  Conow; d 31 Dec 1836  Bresegard
34 Hans Jacob Dien [Hauswirth]: b Abt 1756  ; m 23 Nov 1784  Eldena; d 17 Mar 1816  Bresegard
35 Maria Dorothea Jungbluth: c 18 Sep 1761  Conow
36 Hans Christian Bruening [Hauswirth]: b Abt 1751  ; d  8 Aug 1813  Krohn
37 Catharina Elisabeth Timm: b 10 Jun 1762  Glaisin
38 Johann Hinrich Luetcke [Schulze]: m  5 Dec 1765  ; Gross Laasch
39 Magdalena Charlotte Klaehn: b Balow?
40 Peter Jacob Hinrichs [Hauswirth]: m 24 Nov 1778  ; Conow
41 Lehn Ilse Jacobs

169

```
56 Johann Juergen Stiel: b 1769  Bresegard; m 20 Nov 1798  Bresegard
57 Maria Elisabeth Hinrichs: b 25 Feb 1786  Grebs; d  8 Oct 1815
58 Jochim Christian Hann [Hauswirth]: b 25 Jul 1772  Malk; m 23 Nov 1808  Malk; d  3 Jan 1848  Malk
59 Christina Maria Fehlandt: b 29 Dec 1782  Liepe; d 16 Apr 1858
60 Daniel Hinrich Schroeder: b 1755/1759  Goehren; m 29 Nov 1796  Eldena; d 24 Nov 1832  Glaisin
61 Anna Maria Moeller: b Abt 1777
62 Hans Hinrich Schneider: m 23 Nov 1792  ; Eldena
63 Maria Elisabeth Timm
```

## 7th GENERATION

```
 64 Christian Wiedow
 66 Jacob Friedrich Jungbluth: c 29 Jul 1724  Conow; m 19 Nov 1754  Conow
 67 Anne Margarethe Frarch: b Woosmer?
 68 Hans Jacob Dien: bu 14 Feb 1782  ; Eldena
 69 Maria Haevelman: b Abt 1734  ; d 10 Nov 1809  Bresegardt
 70 Same as individual #66
 71 Same as individual #67
120 Christian Schroeder [Schulze]: b Abt 1718  ; d May 1784  Goehren
121 Maria Ilsabe Ludemann: b Abt 1728  ; d  8 Apr 1797  Goehren
122 Peter Adolph Moeller [Hauswirth]
124 Hans Hinrich Schneider [Hauswirth]
126 Johann Hinrich Timm [Hauswirth]
```

## 8th GENERATION

```
132 Johan Detlov Jungbloht: b Niendorf?; m 16 Nov 1723  Conow
133 Trien Lies Schult: c  1 Jul 1695  Conow
134 Erdmann Frarch
240 Adolph Schroeder [Schulze]
244 Jochim Diederich Moeller
```

## 9th GENERATION

```
266 Andreas Schult: m 13 Nov 1694  ; Conow
267 Eva Gret Jastram: b Wilkenstorf?
```

## 10th GENERATION

```
532 Andreas Schult
534 Geert Jastram
```

170

# Appendix G

# THE GILLHOFF FAMILY

This appendix begins with my words at the grave of Johannes Gillhoff in Ludwigslust on the occasion of the Gillhoff Days in 2002. These words are followed by an Ahnentafel for Johannes Gillhoff – to the extent that the data are known to me. Note that four generations of his paternal ancestors were Lehrer (teachers), and that his great grandfather Johan Juergen Schuett was Schulmeister (schoolmaster). The Ahnentafel is followed by a family group record for "the old schoolteacher" Gottlieb Gillhoff, which chart places the several family members mentioned in the Gillhoff letters (Chapters 4 and 5) in perspective. The appendix closes with descendancy charts for Johann Gillhoff, arbitrarily terminated at generation 9, and Johan Juergen Schuett, arbitrarily terminated at generation 5. The latter chart helps to clarify the first-cousin relationship between Gottlieb Gillhoff and Dorothea (Schuett) Roesch. One finds here the German occupational terms (in addition to those found in Appendix A) Lehrer (teacher), Kuester (sexton), Schulmeister (schoolmaster), Arbeitsmann (workman), Bauer (farmer) and Schneider (tailor). The Gillhoff Ahnentafel was assembled largely by Rolf Gödecke with friendly assistance from the Gillhoff family.

## Johannes Gillhoff (1861-1930)

We have gathered once again to remember and celebrate the life of our beloved Johannes Gillhoff, born 141 years ago in Glaisin and died 72 years ago in Parchim. We remember him especially for his contributions to the preservation of Mecklenburg folklore – as a writer of Mecklenburg folk literature and as editor of the Mecklenburgische Monatshefte (Mecklenburg Monthly). His best-known literary contribution is "Jürnjakob Swehn, der Amerikafahrer" (Jürnjakob Swehn, Emigrant to America), based largely on letters written by an Iowa farmer to his former schoolteacher in Glaisin, Gottlieb Gillhoff, father of Johannes. We have shown that the primary letter writer was a Carl Wiedow, who lived 13 years in the same county in Iowa where I was born and raised. The best-known chapter in this book is "Am Sterbebett der Mutter" (At the Deathbed of my Mother). In my library, I have well-used copies of two readers, "Hannoversches Lesebuch," (The Hannover Reader), 1927 edition, and "Lesebuch für preußische Mittelschulen" (Reader for Prussian Middle Schools), 1928 edition. Both readers contain Gillhoff's "Am Sterbebett der Mutter." From these readers, pupils from all over Germany became acquainted with Jürnjakob Swehn and Johannes Gillhoff. This chapter was written entirely by Johannes Gillhoff – it was not a letter from Iowa edited by Gillhoff. In his recollections of conversations with Gillhoff during Gillhoff's last year, published two months after Gillhoff's death, H.K.A. Krüger writes that "we turned also to talking about the chapter on the mother's death, concerning which I stressed the simplicity and avoided all sentimentality. I feel that is the best of all his works.

"Yes, that was for me also the most effort. The first draft didn't satisfy me at all. Gradually it came to me. It went through five or six drafts."

"Is that about Wiedow's mother?"

"No. He did indeed have his mother come over. But a part of the material is from over there. Then the death of my mother; I arrived just at the right time for the last night watch with her. And then I also wove into the chapter descriptions which I had heard in the family. The welding together did indeed give me much trouble. Hence the many drafts. As a result, this chapter became the best known and did the most for the book, for it was reprinted many times."

When I first read this chapter, I tried to identify Jürnjakob Swehn's mother from the death date and year implied by Jürnjakob's statement, "Last Wednesday, the twelfth of April, I buried my mother." An examination of the burial records recorded for Clayton County, Iowa on that date and day was fruitless. After learning that Gillhoff had his mother on his mind when writing this chapter, I noted that "Wednesday, the twelfth of April" fits the burial date of his mother, namely Wednesday, the twelfth of April, 1905. In the book, we find also that Jürnjakob's mother died at the age of 72 years, 6 months and 5 days. Gillhoff's mother was buried 70 years, 6 months and 5 days after she was born.

With the help of the description given by Werner Schnoor in his 1977 article, "Auf den Spuren des Jürnakob Swehn" (On the Trail of Jürnjakob Swehn), I visited the graves of Johannes Gillhoff's father and mother for the first time in 1990. Their final resting place is in a field bordering on the Glaisin cemetery. The inscription for his father, Gottlieb Gillhoff, says that he was a teacher in Glaisin from 1854 until 1908, that he was born in 1832 in Glaisin and that he died in 1915 in Bremen. My first visit to Johannes Gillhoff's grave had to wait until 1997; I found it with the help of a distant cousin, Lisbeth Künzel, who lived for many years here in Ludwigslust and who I met by chance in Ludwigslust in 1990.

In my library, I have also a small collection of various editions of "Jürnjakob Swehn," some of them showing more wear and tear than others. Incidentally, the most-used copy of the book which I have seen is in the parsonage at Eldena. Obviously that book has been taken from the shelf and read thousands of times. In one of the books in my library is an inscription from a mother to her son, dated 8 December 1958. I would like to close today with this inscription: "It is good for one to be happy in his heart, said my dear old friend Jürnjakob. May you be happy in your heart, my dear Carsten, and grow as fond of this friend as has your mother." Amen.

## 1st GENERATION

1 Johannes Heinrich Carl Christian Gillhoff: b 24 May 1861  Glaisin; d 16 Jan 1930  Parchim

## 2nd GENERATION

2 Georg Gottlieb Johann Heinrich Gillhoff [Lehrer]: b 23 Nov 1832  Glaisin; m 23 May 1856  Eldena; d 13 Jan
  1915  Bremen
3 Helmina Maria Friederica Martens: b  7 Oct 1834  Borgfeld bei Stavenhagen; d  8 Apr 1905  Glaisin

## 3rd GENERATION

4 Johann Christian Peter Gillhoff [Lehrer]: b 24 Aug 1800  Matzlow; m 18 Jul 1828  Eldena; d 12 Jun 1853
  Glaisin
5 Maria Dorothea Schuett: b 14 Feb 1799  Karenz; d 10 Dec 1863  Glaisin
6 Johann Friedrich Martens [Organist und Kuester]: b 1808  ; d 1861
7 Karoline Libnow: d 1882

## 4th GENERATION

8 Hans Joachim Christian Gillhoff [Lehrer]: b 17 Oct 1777  Matzlow; m  8 Nov 1799  ; d 11 Oct 1842  Matzlow
9 Anna Maria Lietz: b 29 Sep 1781  Matzlow; d 25 Dec 1833  Matzlow
10 Johan Juergen Schuett [Schulmeister]
11 Anna Margaretha Catharina Mau

## 5th GENERATION

16 Caspar Christian Gillhoff [Lehrer]: b 23 Jul 1734  Spornitz; m 26 Oct 1759  ; d 1818  Matzlow
17 Catharina Dorothea Missfeld
18 Friedrich L. Lietz [Arbeitsmann und Hauswirth]

## 6th GENERATION

32 Jochim Gillhoff [Bauer]: b 14 Oct 1689  Spornitz; m 21 Nov 1724  ; d  6 Aug 1754  Spornitz
33 Ann Elisabeth Moeller: b  2 Aug 1701  Spornitz; d Oct 1777  Spornitz
34 Johann Missfeld [Tageloehner]

## 7th GENERATION

64 Johann Gillhoff [Bauer]: m 1681
65 Maria Ahrens
66 Jochim Moeller [Hauswirth und Schneider]

## 8th GENERATION

128 Johann Gillhoff [Schultze]
129 Anna Schroeder
130 Ahrens [Hausmann]

## 9th GENERATION

258 Jochim Schroeder [Bauer]

174

**HUSBAND** Georg Gottlieb Johann Heinrich Gillhoff [Lehrer]

| | | |
|---|---|---|
| BIRTH: | 23 Nov 1832 | PLACE: Glaisin |
| CHR.: | 25 Nov 1832 | PLACE: Eldena |
| MAR.: | 23 May 1856 | PLACE: Eldena |
| DEATH: | 13 Jan 1915 | PLACE: Bremen |
| BURIAL: | | PLACE: Glaisin |

Parent Link Type: (B)

FATHER: Johann Christian Peter Gillhoff [Lehrer]    MOTHER: Maria Dorothea Schuett
OTHER WIVES:

**WIFE**  Helmina Maria Friederica Martens

| | | |
|---|---|---|
| BIRTH: | 7 Oct 1834 | PLACE: Borgfeld bei Stavenhagen |
| CHR.: | | PLACE: |
| DEATH: | 8 Apr 1905 | PLACE: Glaisin |
| BURIAL: | 12 Apr 1905 | PLACE: Glaisin |

Parent Link Type: (B)

FATHER: Johann Friedrich Martens [Organist und Kuester]    MOTHER: Karoline Libnow
OTHER HUSBANDS:

**CHILDREN**

1. NAME: Friedrich Wilhelm Ludwig Gillhoff                    Parent Link Type: (B)

| | | |
|---|---|---|
| --- BIRTH: | 7 Apr 1857 | PLACE: Glaisin |
| M CHR.: | | PLACE: |
| MAR.: | | PLACE: |
| DEATH: | 1947 | PLACE: |
| BURIAL: | | PLACE: |

SPOUSE: Magdalene Flass

2. NAME: Gottlieb Ludwig Theodor Johann Gillhoff [Lehrer]     Parent Link Type: (B)

| | | |
|---|---|---|
| --- BIRTH: | 25 Jun 1859 | PLACE: Glaisin |
| M CHR.: | 10 Jul 1859 | PLACE: Eldena |
| MAR.: | 11 Nov 1892 | PLACE: Neustadt |
| DEATH: | 1903 | PLACE: |
| BURIAL: | | PLACE: |

SPOUSE: Auguste Johanna Luise Rehberg

3. NAME: Johannes Heinrich Carl Christian Gillhoff            Parent Link Type: (B)

| | | |
|---|---|---|
| --- BIRTH: | 24 May 1861 | PLACE: Glaisin |
| M CHR.: | 4 Jun 1861 | PLACE: Eldena |
| MAR.: | | PLACE: |
| DEATH: | 16 Jan 1930 | PLACE: Parchim |
| BURIAL: | | PLACE: Ludwigslust |

SPOUSE:

4. NAME: Carl Ludwig Friederich Wilhelm Gillhoff             Parent Link Type: (B)

| | | |
|---|---|---|
| --- BIRTH: | 6 Apr 1863 | PLACE: Glaisin |
| M CHR.: | | PLACE: |
| MAR.: | | PLACE: |
| DEATH: | 1945 | PLACE: |
| BURIAL: | | PLACE: |

SPOUSE:

5. NAME: Carl Gustav Friedrich Heinrich Gillhoff             Parent Link Type: (B)

| | | |
|---|---|---|
| --- BIRTH: | 27 Jul 1865 | PLACE: Glaisin |
| M CHR.: | | PLACE: |
| MAR.: | 1 Oct 1897 | PLACE: Spornitz |
| DEATH: | 1944 | PLACE: |
| BURIAL: | | PLACE: |

SPOUSE: Helene Bruesehafer

6. NAME: Helene Sophie Caroline Dorothea Gillhoff            Parent Link Type: (B)

| | | |
|---|---|---|
| --- BIRTH: | 14 Jun 1867 | PLACE: Glaisin |
| F CHR.: | | PLACE: |
| MAR.: | | PLACE: |
| DEATH: | 6 Jan 1871 | PLACE: Glaisin |
| BURIAL: | | PLACE: |

SPOUSE:

Records of: Eldon L. Knuth
            18085 Boris Drive
            Encino, CA 91316
            USA

Parent Link Types: (B)=Biological, (A)=Adopted, (G)=Guardian, (C)=Challenged, (D)=Disproved

HUSBAND Georg Gottlieb Johann Heinrich Gillhoff [Lehrer]                                          Yr of Birth 1832
WIFE    Helmina Maria Friederica Martens                                                          Yr of Birth 1834

**CHILDREN (continued)**

```
 7. NAME: Theodor Friedrich Carl Johann Gillhoff [Lehrer]                    Parent Link Type: (B)
--- BIRTH:  15 Oct 1869        PLACE: Glaisin
 M  CHR.;                       PLACE:
    MAR.;                       PLACE:
    DEATH:  1959               PLACE:
    BURIAL:                     PLACE:
    SPOUSE: Mary Joergine Jensine Olsen
```

HUSBAND  Georg Gottlieb Johann Heinrich Gillhoff [Lehrer]

WIFE     Helmina Maria Friederica Martens

CHILD 1  Friedrich Wilhelm Ludwig Gillhoff

CHILD 2  Gottlieb Ludwig Theodor Johann Gillhoff [Lehrer]

CHILD 3  Johannes Heinrich Carl Christian Gillhoff

CHILD 4  Carl Ludwig Friederich Wilhelm Gillhoff

CHILD 5  Carl Gustav Friedrich Heinrich Gillhoff

CHILD 6  Helene Sophie Caroline Dorothea Gillhoff

CHILD 7  Theodor Friedrich Carl Johann Gillhoff [Lehrer]

```
     Name          (Birth/Chr.-Death/Burial)   Birth/Chr. Place

1-- Johann Gillhoff [Schultze] (    -    )
 sp-Anna Schroeder (    -    )
   2-- Johann Gillhoff [Bauer] (    -    )
    sp-Maria Ahrens (    -    )
       3-- Jochim Gillhoff [Bauer] (1689-1754)  Spornitz
        sp-Ann Elisabeth Moeller (1701-1777)  Spornitz
           4-- Caspar Christian Gillhoff [Lehrer] (1734-1818)  Spornitz
            sp-Catharina Dorothea Missfeld (    -    )
               5-- Hans Joachim Christian Gillhoff [Lehrer] (1777-1842)  Matzlow
                sp-Anna Maria Lietz (1781-1833)  Matzlow
                   6-- Johann Christian Peter Gillhoff [Lehrer] (1800-1853)  Matzlow
                    sp-Maria Dorothea Schuett (1799-1863)  Karenz
                       7-- Auguste Anna Maria Dorothea Gillhoff (1830-1863)  Glaisin
                       7-- Georg Gottlieb Johann Heinrich Gillhoff [Lehrer] (1832-1915)  Glaisin
                        sp-Helmina Maria Friederica Martens (1834-1905)  Borgfeld bei Stavenhagen
                           8-- Friedrich Wilhelm Ludwig Gillhoff (1857-1947)  Glaisin
                            sp-Magdalene Plass (1860-1937)  Serrahn
                               9-- Magdalene Gillhoff (1889-    )  Schwaan
                               9-- Johannes Gillhoff (1892-    )  Gehlsdorf bei Rostock
                           8-- Gottlieb Ludwig Theodor Johann Gillhoff [Lehrer] (1859-1903)  Glaisin
                            sp-Auguste Johanna Luise Rehberg (1866-1941)  Klein Laasch
                               9-- Martha Marie Helene Gillhoff (1893-    )
                               9-- Friedrich Karl Johannes Gillhoff (1894-    )  Raddenfort
                               9-- Karl August Erich Friedrich Gillhoff (1896-1899)  Raddenfort
                               9-- Marie Anna Klara Sophie Gillhoff (1898-    )  Raddenfort
                           8-- Johannes Heinrich Carl Christian Gillhoff (1861-1930)  Glaisin
                           8-- Carl Ludwig Friederich Wilhelm Gillhoff (1863-1945)  Glaisin
                           8-- Carl Gustav Friedrich Heinrich Gillhoff (1865-1944)  Glaisin
                            sp-Helene Bruesehafer (1872-    )  Spornitz
                               9-- Margareta Frieda Helmine Luise Berta Gillhoff (1898-    )  Schwaan
                               9-- Gerhard Gillhoff (1901-    )  Schwaan
                               9-- Eva-Maria Johanna Paula Frieda Gillhoff (1904-    )  Schwaan
                               9-- Erika Magdalena Theodora Johanna Gillhoff (1906-    )  Schwaan
                           8-- Helene Sophie Caroline Dorothea Gillhoff (1867-1871)  Glaisin
                           8-- Theodor Friedrich Carl Johann Gillhoff [Lehrer] (1869-1959)  Glaisin
                            sp-Mary Joergine Jensine Olsen (1874-    )
                               9-- Gunnar Gottlieb Gustav Gillhoff (1902-    )  Gehlsdorf bei Rostock
                               9-- Willi Gillhoff (1904-1905)  Gehlsdorf bei Rostock
                               9-- Gerd Karl Wilhelm Aage Gillhoff (1906-    )  Gehlsdorf bei Rostock
                       7-- Louise Amalia Maria Gillhoff (1834-1892)  Glaisin
                       7-- Carl Johannes Christian Gillhoff (1837-1837)  Glaisin
                       7-- Catharina Wilhelmina Lucia Gillhoff (1838-1894)  Glaisin
   2-- Dorothea Gillhoff (1673-1760)
```

177

| Name | (Birth/Chr.-Death/Burial) | Birth/Chr. Place |
|------|---------------------------|------------------|

```
1-- Johan Juergen Schuett [Schulmeister] (   -   )
 sp-Anna Margaretha Catharina Mau (   -   )
   2-- Johan Christian Schuett (   -   )
    sp-Anna Elisabeth Bruening (   -   )
      3-- Carolina Maria Dorothea Lucia Schuett (1836-1921)  Glaisin
       sp-Johann Juergen Heinrich Roesch (1831-1895)  Glaisin
         4-- Wilhelmina Catharina Elisabeth Roesch (1862-1918)  Glaisin
          sp-Ludwig Schlesselman (   -   )
         4-- Maria Sophia Johanna Roesch (1864-1904)  Glaisin
         4-- Elisabeth Maria Wilhelmina Roesch (1867-1904)  Glaisin
          sp-Henry Koehn (   -   )
         4-- Caroline J. Roesch (1869-1889)  Iowa
         4-- Ludwig Friedrich Heinrich Roesch (1872-1924)  Iowa County, Iowa
          sp-Lena Agnes Myers (   -   )
         4-- Anna Roesch (1874-1950)  Iowa County, Iowa
          sp-Charles Timmerman (   -   )
            5-- Emil Timmerman (1894-1954)
             sp-Lucy Roggentine (   -   )
            5-- Rena Timmerman (1896-1983)
             sp-John W. Fruendt (   -   )
            5-- Laura Timmerman (1903-1969)
            5-- Raymond Timmerman (1911-   )
             sp-Johnita Timmerman (   -   )
            5-- Ione Timmerman (   -   )
         4-- Heinrich R. Roesch (1878-1889)
   2-- Maria Dorothea Schuett (1799-1863)
    sp-Johann Christian Peter Gillhoff [Lehrer] (1800-1853)  Malchow
      3-- Auguste Anna Maria Dorothea Gillhoff (1830-1863)  Glaisin
      3-- Georg Gottlieb Johann Heinrich Gillhoff [Lehrer] (1832-1915)  Glaisin
       sp-Helmina Maria Friederica Martens (1834-1905)  Borgfeld bei Stavenhagen
         4-- Friedrich Wilhelm Ludwig Gillhoff (1857-1947)  Glaisin
          sp-Magdalene (   -   )
            5-- Johannes Gillhoff (   -   )
            5-- Magdalene Gillhoff (   -   )
         4-- Gottlieb Ludwig Theodor Johann Gillhoff [Lehrer] (1859-1903)  Glaisin
          sp-Auguste Johanne Luise Rehberg (1866-1941)  Klein Laasch
            5-- Martha Gillhoff (1893-   )
         4-- Johannes Heinrich Carl Christian Gillhoff (1861-1930)  Glaisin
         4-- Carl Ludwig Friederich Wilhelm Gillhoff (1863-1945)  Glaisin
         4-- Carl Gustov Friedrich Heinrich Gillhoff (1865-1944)  Glaisin
         4-- Helene Sophie Caroline Dorothea Gillhoff (1867-1871)  Glaisin
         4-- Theodor Friedrich Carl Johann Gillhoff [Lehrer] (1869-1959)  Glaisin
          sp-Mary Olsen (1874-   )
            5-- Gerd Gillhoff (   -   )
            5-- Gunnar Gillhoff (   -   )
      3-- Louise Amalia Maria Gillhoff (1834-1892)  Glaisin
      3-- Carl Johannes Christian Gillhoff (1837-1837)  Glaisin
      3-- Catharina Wilhelmina Lucia Gillhoff (1838-1894)  Glaisin
   2-- Carolina Sophia Maria Schuett (1805-1806)  Glaisin
```

178

# Appendix H

# THE AUTHOR

The author was born and grew up in Clayton County, Iowa. Clayton County was the goal of many immigrants from Mecklenburg during the last half of the 19th century. If one considers both his adopted family (Knuth - Becker) and his birth family (Koevenig - Oldag) one finds that 15 of his ancestors emigrated from either Mecklenburg or Vorpommern. (See the table at the end of this appendix.) In his early years, the everyday language of the community was "Mecklenburger Platt" (a low-German dialect); he learned English in school. After one term of college, he was drafted and spent two years in the U.S. Army, including combat duty in France. His combat duties culminated when he was trapped for five days behind the German lines in winter weather and acquired a foot and leg condition known as trench foot. He received a medical discharge and resumed his studies, finishing at the California Institute of Technology in 1953 with a Ph.D. in Aeronautics. After three years in the Aerospace industry, he joined the University of California at Los Angeles, where he taught and did research in the School of Engineering and Applied Science until his retirement in 1991. He has authored more than 100 scientific publications.

In 1975, Prof. Knuth received from Germany a von Humboldt Senior Scientist Award in honor of his research contributions. This award enabled him to spend a year at the Max-Planck-Institut für Strömungsforschung (Flow Research) in Göttingen, Germany. Since then, he has been an annual guest at the MPI and has visited Germany more than 30 times. He visited Mecklenburg for the first time in 1976, when it was still part of East Germany, and numerous times since. These visits, coupled with his ability to handle the German language, enabled him to do extensive genealogical research, to work with local genealogists and to locate relatives in several areas of Germany.

Prof. Knuth has presented results of his genealogical researches at meetings organized in Iowa by the Iowa Genealogical Society, in Mecklenburg by the Johannes Gillhoff Society and in Burbank by the Immigrant Genealogical Society. Results of these researches have appeared in the <u>Hawkeye Heritage</u>, published quarterly by the Iowa Genealogical Society, in <u>Die Pommerschen Leute</u>, published quarterly in Burbank, California, in <u>Mecklenburg</u>, published monthly in Mecklenburg, and in the <u>Neues Trierisches Jahrbuch</u>, published annually in Trier, Germany. In 1999, the Johannes Gillhoff Society named Prof. Knuth an honorary member; in 2002, the Landsmannschaft Mecklenburg presented him with the Fritz-Reuter Medal and the village of Glaisin, Mecklenburg named him the first honorary citizen of the village of Glaisin. See certificates at end of appendix.

ANCESTORS OF ELDON L. KNUTH
WHO EMIGRATED FROM MECKLENBURG-VORPOMMERN
TO CLAYTON COUNTY, IOWA

<u>Adopted Family</u>

Greatgrandfather:  Carl David Moritz Knuth
born 16.04.1835, Nepsin

Greatgrandmother:  Caroline Auguste Ernestine Dorothee Heiden
born 13.01.1834, Priemen

Grandfather:  Hermann Max Carl Knuth
born 22.04.1863, Upatel

Greatgrandfather:  Joachim Friedrich Heinrich Garms
born 20.09.1822, Göhren

Greatgrandmother:  Katharine Elisabeth Johanna Schult
born 07.08.1829, Grebs

Greatgrandfather:  Johann Heinrich Christoph Becker
born 16.11.1819, Alt Krenzlin

Greatgrandmother:  Catharina Maria Elisabeth Hanna Klähn
born 13.09.1825, Hornkaten

Grandfather:  Heinrich Friedrich Wilhelm Becker
born 22.09.1857, Warlow

## Birth Family

| | |
|---|---|
| Greatgrandfather: | Otto Johann Friedrich Blumhagen<br>born 24.04.1837, Sandhagen |
| Greatgrandmother: | Friedrike Caroline Christina Stoltenburg<br>born 02.03.1838, Kreckow |
| Grandmother: | Christine Johanna Blumhagen<br>born 18.10.1874, Strassburg<br>(Mecklenburg-Strelitz) |
| Greatgrandfather: | Johann Wilhelm Friedrich Peter Oldag<br>born 19.03.1839, Grebs |
| Greatgrandmother: | Sophie Dorothe Elisabeth Föls<br>born 24.10.1838, Marnitz |
| Greatgrandfather: | Johann Joachim Friedrich Koss<br>born 28.11.1834, Alt Lüblow |
| Greatgrandmother: | Elisabeth Maria Friedericke Wilke<br>born 24.05.1841, Lübesse |

## Herrn Prof. Dr. Eldon L. Knuth

wird hiermit in dankbarer Anerkennung
der besonderen Verdienste
für unser Land Mecklenburg

die

# Fritz-Reuter-Medaille

verliehen.

Ratzeburg, *8. Juni 2002*

## Landsmannschaft Mecklenburg

Die Gemeinde Glaisin
verleiht auf der Grundlage des Beschlusses der
Gemeindevertretersitzung vom 31. Mai 2002

## Herrn Prof. Eldon L. Knuth
den Titel
## Ehrenbürger
### der Gemeinde Glaisin

In mühevoller Kleinarbeit hat Prof. Eldon L. Knuth das Urbild des Jürnjakob Swen ermittelt, damit die Gillhoff-Forschung ungemein bereichert und unser Dorf international bekannt gemacht. Seine Forschungsergebnisse veröffentlichte er und hielt mehrere Vorträge zur Migrationsgeschichte auf den Fachtagungen in Glaisin und anderen Orten Deutschlands und Amerikas. Professor Eldon L. Knuth gehört seit vielen Jahren zu den treuesten Freunden unseres Gillhoffdorfes.

Glaisin, den 08. Juni 2002

J. Behrends
Bürgermeister

U. Baarck
Stellv. Bürgermeister

Printed in the United States
36690LVS00005B/352-369

9 781420 834789